10 Minute Guide to Lotus® Notes Mail 4.5

by Jane Calabria with Dorothy Burke

A Division of Macmillan Computer Publishing
201 West 103rd St., Indianapolis, Indiana 46290 USA

Dedicated with gratitude to Tom Barich who introduced me to Que and to Dave Gallagher who introduced me to Lotus Notes.

International Standard Book Number: 0-7897-0974-0

Library of Congress Catalog Card Number: 96-70544

98 8 7 6 5

Interpretation of the printing code: the rightmost number of the first series of numbers is the year of the book's printing; the rightmost number of the second series of numbers is the number of the book's printing. For example, a printing code of 96-1 shows that the first printing of the book occurred in 1996.

Printed in the United States of America

Publisher: Roland Elgey
Editorial Services Director: Elizabeth Keaffaber
Publishing Director: Lynn E. Zingraf
Acquistions Coordinator: Martha O'Sullivan
Managing Editor: Michael Cunningham
Product Development Specialist: Melanie Palaisa
Production Editor: Mark Enochs
Copy Editor: San Dee Phillips
Cover Designer: Dan Armstrong
Book Designer: Barbara Kordesh
Technical Specialist: Nadeem Muhammed
Indexer: Eric Brinkman
Production: Lissa Auciello-Brogan, Troy Barnes, Kathleen Caulfield, Jerry Cole, Trudy Coler, Michelle Croninger, Dana Davis, Toi Davis, Sean Decker, David Faust, Stephanie Hammett, Natalie Hollifield, Kevin J. MacDonald, Heather Pope, Linda Quigley, Karen Teo

Special thanks to Debby Lynd for ensuring the technical accuracy of this book.

Contents

Introduction

I remember a time when it was very hip to have a fax number on one's business card. Then voice mail became very popular and often *two* phone numbers were printed on business cards; the company main number, and a voice mail number. The use of mobile phones began to grow and our mobile phone numbers were given only to those very special clients who felt very special simply because we gave them our precious mobile phone numbers! Now, we add e-mail addresses to our business cards. With the growth of commercial service providers and corporate LANs and WANs , the growth of the Internet and the World Wide Web, and the use of virtual offices, e-mail addresses on business cards are as common as telephone numbers, fax numbers, and voice mail numbers. It might be time for us all to buy stock in companies who manufacture bifocal lenses!

Riding the wave of this growth period is software classified as *groupware* and, in particular, a program called Lotus Notes. Part of the Lotus Notes groupware product is their e-mail program and it is one of the most robust and advanced e-mail programs available today. It's been my pleasure to depend on Lotus Notes Mail as a productivity tool in my career for the past three years. Lotus Notes is an ever evolving product, constantly improving and answering the needs of those of us who depend as strongly on our e-mail as we do on our telephones. It provides a flexible and dependable e-mail product for large and small businesses with a user interface that's not only easy to learn, but down right good looking!

Welcome to the 10 Minute Guide to Lotus Notes Mail

Not everyone has the luxury or the budget to attend classes for the purpose of learning Lotus Notes Mail. This book focuses on the basics of Lotus Notes Mail, introduces general e-mail practices, and shows you some advanced features of the program. You can work through the book lesson by lesson, building upon your skills, or you can use the book as a quick reference when you want to perform a new task. Features and concepts are covered in lessons that take 10 minutes or less to complete.

If you are new to e-mail, start at the beginning of the book. If you've used e-mail before, you might want to skip the first few lessons (but be certain to read about e-mail etiquette) and work from there. If you've been using Lotus Notes Mail, use the Table of Contents and select the lessons that cover features of the program you haven't yet used.

This book can work as a tutorial for you or as a reference for those tasks you seldom perform. If you're traveling with Lotus Notes Mail on your laptop, the compact size of this book is perfect for fitting into your laptop or notebook case.

Who Should Use This Book

The 10 Minute Guide to Lotus Notes Mail is for anyone who:

- Has Lotus Notes, Notes Desktop, or Notes Mail installed on their PC.
- Needs to learn Lotus Notes Mail quickly.
- Wants to explore some of the advanced features of Mail.
- Wants a quick way to select, learn and perform tasks in Lotus Notes Mail.

About the Installation of Lotus Notes

Lotus Notes is not a standalone product. To use Lotus Notes Mail, one must be a registered user in an established private or public Notes domain. Because most people use Notes at work, it is unusual that people like you and I install Notes on our PCs or laptops without help and specific instructions from our Notes System Administrators.

The actual installation of the program is easy, and depending upon the version of Notes (Lotus Notes, Notes Desktop, or Notes Mail) you'll feed as many as 14 disks, or use one CD to install. There are four or five questions which you must answer with very specific details about your organization and your Notes home server. That information regarding the server is different for every organization. Notes support personnel typically install Notes on PCs at the office and do not look to end users to do the install. The exception to the rule may be for laptop or remote users. If your organization relies on you to install the program, they must supply you with the proper information to answer those questions. Since the install is easy and the questions vary, we didn't supply specific installation instructions in this guide. We did, however, start with information about your Notes setup once the program is installed on your PC.

CONVENTIONS USED IN THIS BOOK

With version 4.5 of Lotus Notes, Lotus changed the name of their server software to "Domino," keeping their client software name of "Lotus Notes." Throughout this book, we may universally refer to both the client and server software as "Notes" or "Lotus Notes." Only when it becomes crucially important to differentiate between client and server software do we call the server software "Domino."

Throughout this book are icons that identify tips to help you save time and learn important information fast.

TimeSaver Tips Look for this icon for shortcuts and ideas that will save you time when working in Lotus Notes Mail. Some tips even apply to other Windows based programs!

Panic Button Watch for this icon to give you a heads up on common mistakes or where new users might run into trouble.

Plain English This icon will be used to introduce new terms, or Notes-specific terms.

You also find these conventions throughout the steps in the lessons:

What you type	Things you type with the keyboard appear in **bold, color type**.
What you select	Any keys that you press or items that you select with your mouse appear in color type.
On-screen text	Any messages that you see on-screen appear in **bold type**.

ACKNOWLEDGMENTS

No project is completed by one person, and this project, is no exception. I'd like to thank my Acquisitions Editor, Martha O'Sullivan and my Production Development Specialist, Melanie Palaisa. As a team, their combined talents, coaching, attention to detail, expertise, and humor made every minute of this project enjoyable and challenging. Martha presented this opportunity and Melanie enabled me to grasp it. Thanks to Dorothy Burke whose valuable writing contribution kept us all within our deadlines. I'd also like to thank Denise Prante who questions my every word and keystroke and Patience Rockey for supporting my endeavors outside of the training arena. Finally (though hardly last) I'd like to thank my husband and partner Rob Kirkland—"Dr. Notes"—who makes work, writing, and life an extraordinary experience.

TRADEMARKS

After reading this book, if you would like more information on Lotus Notes, I suggest the following from Que:

The 10 Minute Guide to Lotus Notes 4.5 by Sue Plumley

The 10 Minute Guide to InterNotes Web Navigator by Jane Calabria

Using Lotus Notes 4.5 by Cate Richards

LESSON 1

Understanding Lotus Notes Concepts

In this lesson, you learn about Lotus Notes concepts and how Lotus Notes stores information. You also learn how Lotus Notes presents that stored information to you.

Understanding Clients and Servers

Lotus Notes works on a *client/server* technology. Your PC is the Lotus Notes client. It requests and receives information from the Domino server. In the office, you're "attached" to the server over your network.

You communicate with the Lotus Notes server through a series of wires and cables (hardware) and networking software. The information you request is in Lotus Notes applications, or *databases*. The Domino server usually stores those databases so that they can be accessed by many "clients" at one time. In most cases, when you double-click on a Lotus Notes icon, you are actually opening a database stored on the server. Your client (your PC) requests that database from the server and when the database opens, the database that resides on the server appears (see Figure 1.1).

This figure is like the connection you have at work to your *file server*. You often store work that you create in other software programs (other than Lotus Notes) on the file server on your network at the office. You might create a Lotus 123 spreadsheet or a Word document. When you save those files, you might save them on your drive F:. Your drive F: is actually space dedicated to you for storage on the file server.

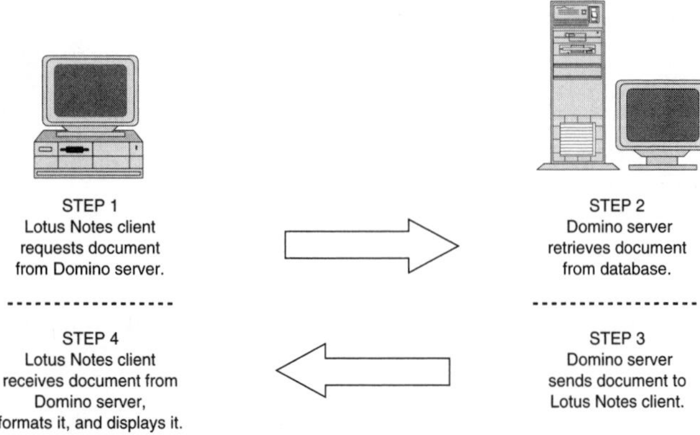

FIGURE 1.1 How clients and servers work.

There are three types of clients available for Lotus Notes: Lotus Notes, Notes Desktop, and Notes Mail. All three of these types include mail.

UNDERSTANDING DATABASES

There are many different uses for Notes databases. One database might hold customer information, while another holds information about company projects, and still another holds your mail. Even your e-mail is a Lotus Notes database. Databases are like little miniprograms or applications. Just like having multiple spreadsheet files with different formulas and calculations for solving various business problems, Notes databases are usually created to solve a specific business process, such as customer service calls, client tracking for sales, or expense reporting.

Although many Notes databases are created by an Application Developer, as mentioned earlier, the Mail database is already created and comes with all three client types of Lotus Notes. If you only have Notes Mail installed, you can only use the Lotus Notes Mail database. If you use Lotus Notes or Lotus Notes Desktop, you have a bigger software program that includes more features than Notes Mail; you can use the *other* Lotus Notes databases for client databases and discussion databases.

The Mail database is different from other Lotus Notes databases you may be using because it is a *private* database for your use only. Others cannot access or use your mail database. On the other hand, other departments or the whole company can access customer databases.

Even though your Mail database is private, it is stored on the Domino 4.5 server. Unless you are a remote (or mobile) user who uses Lotus Notes at a PC at home or on your laptop on the road, you usually don't even have a copy of the Mail database on your PC. All that you have is the icon for the database that, when double-clicked, opens the database on the server.

UNDERSTANDING DOCUMENTS AND FORMS

Lotus Notes database stores everything in *documents* (containers for the data in Notes). Each document that represents data you have entered contains fields for each of the pieces of data you have entered. It's a little weird to say that you never really see these documents but you don't. Documents are like records; and a record contains fields. In this sense, Lotus Notes works like other kinds of databases. What's different about Lotus Notes is that you don't actually *see* the records, or documents. You see contents of the documents by looking at them through *forms*.

Database Record A collection of data entered into fields. Consider the phone book. When you look for a person in the phone book, you look for the information that has to do with a specific individual. That information is the name, address, and phone number, which would be considered ***fields***. All of the information for that individual is a ***record,*** and all of the records in the phone book combined is the database.

Every database in Lotus Notes has custom forms designed for use within that database. The Lotus Notes Mail database is no exception. In the Mail database, there are many forms. The ones you'll use the most are the Memo, Reply, Calendar Entry and Task forms. These forms contain fields such as the To: field and the Subject field. It's not important to memorize all the fields and forms but it is good to understand that you work in fields and forms (see Figure 1.2).

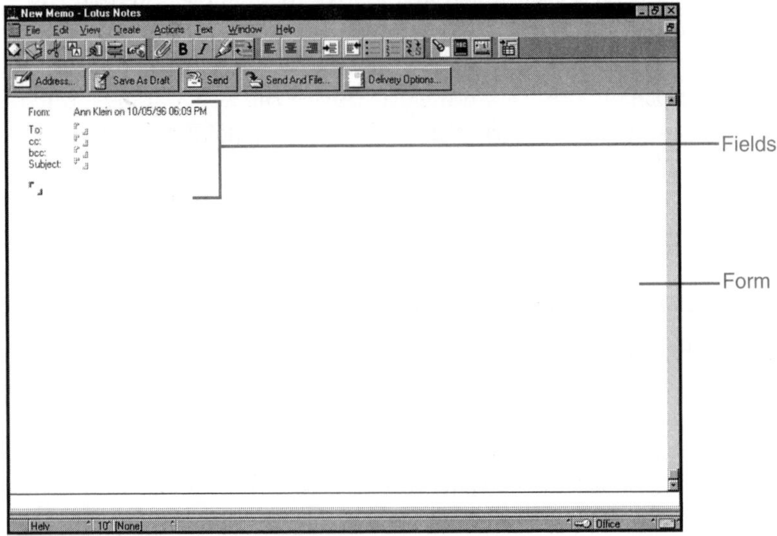

FIGURE 1.2 The Mail Memo form.

UNDERSTANDING VIEWS

Now that you know you have fields of information stored in records (documents) that you see through forms, you can see a list of documents by looking at a *view*. The view acts like a table of contents listing the documents in your Mail database. Your Inbox is nothing more than a view listing the documents (mail) you've received (see Figure 1.3). When you want to read your mail, double-click on the piece of mail in the view and you will read your mail in a form.

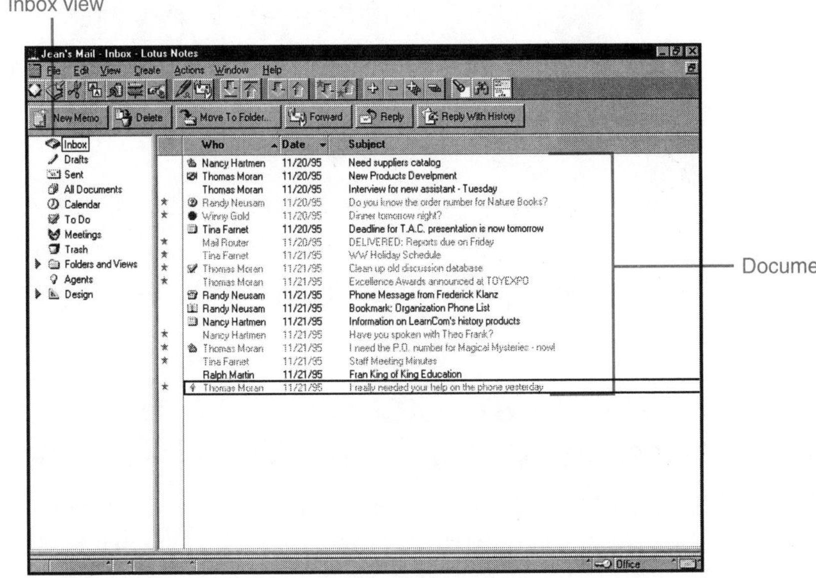

FIGURE 1.3 The Inbox View listing documents.

In this lesson, you learned about clients and servers. You also learned about Lotus Notes databases and how Lotus Notes displays the contents of its databases. In the next lesson, you learn more specifics about the Mail database.

LESSON 2

How Lotus Notes Mail Works

In this lesson, you learn about e-mail, Lotus Notes Mail, and e-mail etiquette.

Sending and Receiving Mail: Company-Wide and World-Wide

E-mail is short for electronic mail. Simply put, it's mail that you create on your computer and send to someone over a network. With Lotus Notes, you create a mail memo. When you click the Send button, the mail travels to the server and into the mailbox of the addressee(s). When they open their mail, they see the mail you sent. With Lotus Notes, the Domino server stores all the mailboxes of the users on the Domino server.

Your Domino server may have access to the Internet. If it does, then you can send mail to people on the Internet. You need to make sure that you address the mail properly (as described in Lesson 6). Mail that you send to the Internet first travels to your Domino server and then to the Internet from the server. This might happen immediately or it might be on a scheduled basis depending upon how your administrator configured your Domino server.

It's possible that you can send e-mail to other people who have Lotus Notes Mail or cc:Mail but are not using the same server as you. This depends upon the way your administrator sets up the Domino server. This doesn't necessarily mean that if you have Lotus Notes Mail at work you can send e-mail to your cousin across the country, even though she has Lotus Notes Mail at her job. However, if your company and her company have reason to send mail back and forth, they can have their servers call each other and send and receive mail. If that's the case, you can send mail to your cousin.

It's more likely that you work in a large company that has several Domino servers located in several different departments. In order to have mail distributed company-wide, those servers must talk to each other and exchange mail messages. Then you can send mail to someone on another Domino server.

Using E-mail Etiquette

Because so many people use e-mail, it's necessary to have certain "rules" that all users follow. E-mail began in corporations and businesses whose employees needed to communicate with each other quickly and efficiently. Since e-mail was originally a business program, the people who used it developed business rules and guidelines: What's proper; what's not. What's acceptable; what's grounds for getting in trouble. This is *e-mail etiquette*. Some of these ideas and concepts will make perfect sense to you; with others, you may ask "Why?"

Check out these points of etiquette so you can responsibly and effectively use Lotus Notes Mail. Remember that many large corporations have company policies regarding e-mail; ask your company for a copy of these policies. Breaking of company policies can, in some situations, result in loosing your job.

Always Include Information in the Subject Line

Don't send a piece of e-mail without including something in the Subject line. Why not? When you look in your Inbox to see your list of mail, you'll see a list that includes who the mail is from, the date of the mail, and the subject. If you leave your subject line blank, it will be blank in the recipients Inbox.

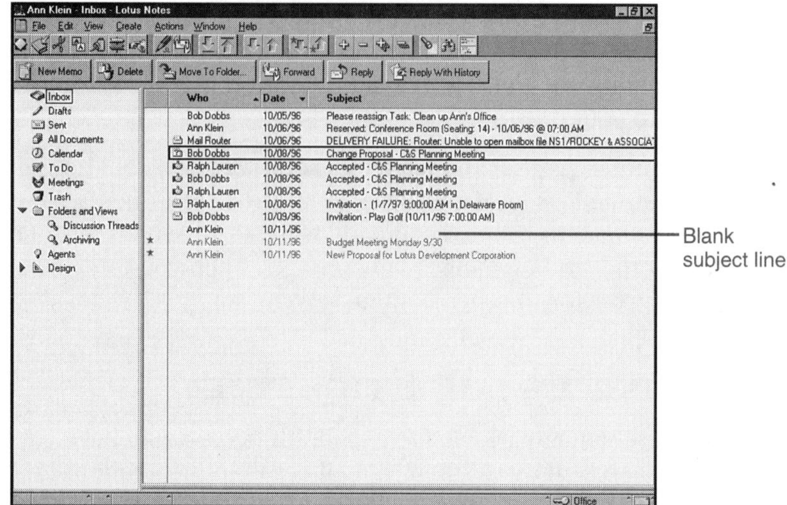

FIGURE 2.1 A blank subject line provides little information to the recipient.

Do you have voice mail? Or an answering machine? Say you've been out of the office for a day or so. You return to find 10 voice mails waiting for you, and somewhere in the middle is a message from someone saying "Hi, it's me; give me a call." You don't know the time, date, or subject of the call—or the name of the caller. So, how can you return this call? When you leave telephone or e-mail messages, be thoughtful and efficient; avoid leaving meaningless messages.

When you send messages by e-mail, fill in the e-mail Subject line. Make that line of information clear and concise.

BEWARE OF THE WRITTEN WORD

If you're not willing to post your message by the water cooler, maybe you should think twice about e-mailing it. Although e-mail is fairly secure, it's not entirely secure. Someone might forward your message to others. Sarcasm doesn't translate well from the spoken word to the written word. You might be taken seriously or offend someone when you were only joking. And if you fail to spell check your e-mail, you may be thought of as something less than the brilliant person you know you are.

SEND E-MAIL THAT HAS MEANING

Some companies do not allow any personal use of e-mail. Maybe your company doesn't mind you using e-mail to ask someone to join you for lunch or to ask if she's going to the company softball game. Be thoughtful, however, about the number of messages you send people and the importance of those messages. People who use e-mail extensively for work might not appreciate unsolicited jokes, thoughts for the day, gossip, and cartoons. E-mail is a tool to help people work more productively.

DON'T PRINT OUT YOUR INBOX

This is not exactly an etiquette issue, it's more a common sense issue. If you print your e-mail for reading purposes, aren't you defeating the purpose? Why not have people send everything to you on paper to begin with? Avoid being counterproductive.

GIVE THOUGHT TO SENDING ATTACHMENTS

You can send attachments of other files from other programs within your Lotus Notes Mail. This is a fantastic tool, but don't forget that within Windows products you can cut, copy, and paste information from one program to another.

If you attach a file, then the recipient has to start another program to read that file. That can take time out of his working day. Send an attachment only if the recipient needs to make changes to or have a copy of that file for his records. Also send an attachment if the information you are distributing is a large amount of information. For paragraphs, and small tables, and small amounts of text, use cut, copy, and paste to put that information directly into the body of your mail memo.

When sending attachments, include information so the receiver knows what the file contains *before* he opens it. A simple line such as "Please read the attached" is not descriptive enough. A simple line such as "This is the spreadsheet for the third quarter budget" is much more descriptive and helpful.

Don't Send E-Mail to the World

Don't create large distribution lists. If you're responsible for sending out policy changes, you can store those policy changes in a Notes database. If you need to send the same e-mail message to massive distribution lists, ask your Notes administrator for their advice. You might need a *discussion* database application or a *repository* application. These types of databases might be better than using the Mail database for sharing information.

DON'T USE ALL CAPS

That title seems too strong, doesn't it? That's because typing in all uppercase letters implies that you're shouting. Most computer users think shouting is impolite.

Use Reply to All

When you answer an e-mail message, you can reply to the sender, or reply to the sender and all of the people that the sender included in the original mail. Maybe the sender cc'd (copied) several people or had several names in the To: field. If your answer would be of use to the others in the original list, please remember to use the Reply to All feature. Otherwise, the poor person who sent you the e-mail may have to take your reply and resend it to the others they were trying to include from the start.

Keep Your Messages Short

The shorter the better. Some people often skip over an e-mail when the message contains more than a screen full of information. They might think, "I'll read this later when I have more time." E-mail is often forgotten because of exactly that thought, so keep it short and your message will be read.

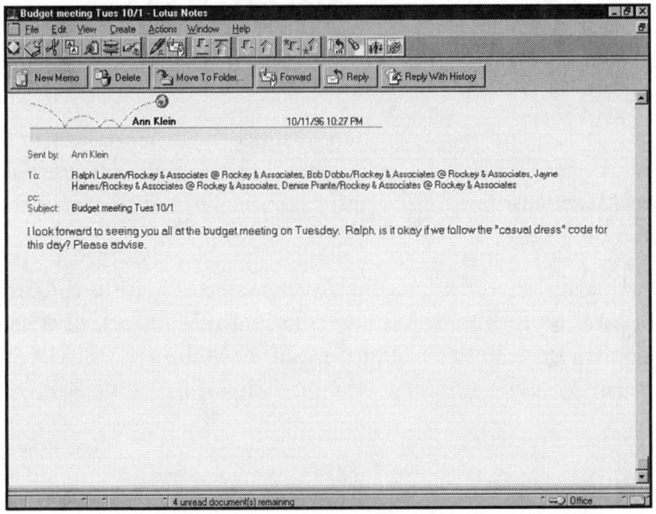

Figure 2.2 This message needs a "Reply to All."

Remember That You Are Using Company Property

Your company purchased the computer on which you are working. Your company purchased the software you are using to send mail. And your company (hopefully) is paying you during the time you spend to write your mail messages. Sounds as if this is company property, doesn't it? It's a good idea to treat your mail like company property. If your topic is too personal, not work related, or highly confidential, it might not be an appropriate piece of e-mail.

In this lesson, you learned some pointers for proper use of e-mail. You also learned not to "shout" and to keep your messages short, but meaningful. In the next lesson you'll learn about the workspace.

LESSON 3

USING THE WORKSPACE

In this lesson, you learn how to move around the Lotus Notes workspace. You also learn how to read the status bar and customize workspace page tabs.

To start Lotus Notes and access the workspace, double-click the Lotus Notes icon in your Windows Program Manager, or select Lotus Notes from your Programs menu in Windows 95. The Notes workspace appears, similar to the one shown in Figure 3.1.

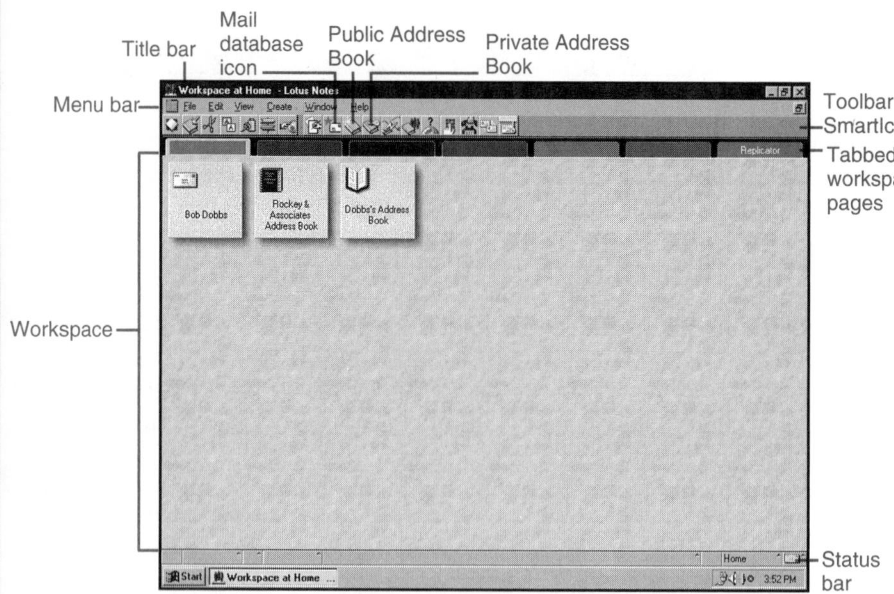

FIGURE 3.1 The Lotus Notes workspace.

Your workspace probably looks like the workspace in Figure 3.1. This is what a workspace would look like if you just installed Lotus Notes. You would see your Lotus Notes Mail database icon and icons for your Public and Private Address Books.

The Lotus Notes workspace in Figure 3.1 looks similar to and acts much like other programs you use in Windows:

- The *title bar* shows the current location page and the program name.
- The *menu bar* has all of the menu selections for this window, so the menu bar will change, depending upon the Notes window that is active. When you click a menu name, a submenu displays all the commands associated with that menu item. As in Windows, if a command is dimmed or gray, it is not currently available.
- The *toolbar* contains icons you can use in lieu of using the menu; Lotus calls these icons *SmartIcons* (more about these icons later in the lesson).
- The *workspace* has several tabbed pages. This helps you organize your work. You can put different database icons on different pages (you'll learn how later in this lesson). To move from one tabbed page to another, simply click the tab of the page you want to see. The page moves to the front and becomes the "active" workspace page.
- The *status bar* appears at the bottom of the screen. It contains information such as your location (in Figure 3.1, this is home) and gives you access to your mail, which you'll learn more about in Lesson 4.

Shortcut Keys You can quickly access commands in the menu bar by pressing the Alt key and the underlined letter of the menu or command name. For example, Alt+F will have the same effect as clicking with your mouse on the word File.

Working on the Road? If you use Lotus Notes remotely (away from the office on your laptop or your PC at home), you must change your location. See Lesson 23 to learn how to set up Notes to work remotely.

CUSTOMIZING WORKSPACE PAGES

One of the first things you might want to do in planning the organization of your workspace is to give names to your workspace pages. There are probably eight workspace pages on your workspace right now. You can put names on the tabs, select the color for the tab, and add new tabbed pages whenever you need more. To further organize your information, you can also move database icons from one workspace page to another.

NAMING TABS AND CHANGING TAB COLORS

To name a tab or change its color, follow these steps:

1. With your *right* mouse button click the tab of the current page (see Figure 3.2).

FIGURE 3.2 Workspace tab of current page.

2. A pop-up menu appears. Select Workspace Properties.
3. The Properties box appears, as shown in Figure 3.3. In the Workspace page name: text box, type the name of the database. For this example, type **Mail**. (Reserve this page strictly for your Mail database and your Address Book databases during the rest of the lessons in this book.)

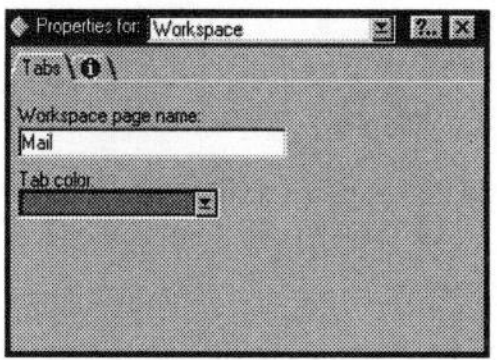

FIGURE 3.3 The Properties box.

4. To change the color of the tab, click the Tab color: drop-down menu. Click a color you like.
5. To close this dialog box and save your changes, click the Close (X) button in the upper right corner of the Properties box. You can now see your newly named tab.

Even though you have changed the color of a tab, the page itself does not change color. The page that is active, or in front, is always gray; it's the tab colors that help differentiate between pages.

If you do have other databases and you want to organize them into separate workspace pages, simply name the tabs on your other workspace pages in preparation for moving your database icons to those pages (you'll learn how to move database icons next).

MOVING A DATABASE ICON TO A DIFFERENT WORKSPACE PAGE

If you have no other database icons on your workspace, you can experiment with moving database icons by using your Mail icon.

However, when you finish moving the icon, move it back to the original workspace page. To move a database icon follow these steps:

1. Click the database icon to select it.
2. Drag the icon to the tab of the new workspace page where you want this icon to appear.
3. When a square appears around the tab of the new workspace page, release the mouse button (see Figure 3.4).
4. Your icon should no longer appear on your current workspace page.
5. Click the new workspace page tab, and you will see your database icon.

FIGURE 3.4 Moving a database icon.

ADDING TABS TO THE WORKSPACE

1. Select Create, Workspace page from the menu.
2. The new workspace tab is added to your workspace.
3. With your right mouse button, click the new workspace tab.
4. Select Workspace Properties from the pop-up menu.
5. Name the page and select a color for the tab in the Properties box.
6. Close the Properties box and save your changes.

CHANGING THE INFORMATION DISPLAYED ON A DATABASE ICON

Your database icons can provide information about how many unread documents you have in the database, the name of the database and where you can find the database (on the Domino server or on your hard drive, "on local").

- To display the number of unread documents, choose View, Show Unread from the menu.
- To display the location of the database, choose View, Show Server Names. If the database is on your server, your server name will appear on the icon. If the database is on your hard drive (likely if you are a remote or mobile user), on Local appears on the icon as its location.
- To display the file name of the database, hold down the Shift key while selecting View, Show Server Names. This will turn off the server name and display the file name.
- To display both the location of the database and the file name, hold down the Shift key while selecting View, Show Server Names.

USING SMARTICONS

SmartIcons (a Lotus term) are the icons located on the toolbar. Most of your Windows products contain a toolbar with icons that act as shortcuts or alternatives to using the menu. Some people find it faster to click a SmartIcon than to look through the menus to find choices such as opening a database or bolding text. The SmartIcons change as you work in different parts of Lotus Notes.

Lotus Notes helps you to understand the function of each SmartIcon with a feature that shows the SmartIcons description. To see this brief description, hold your mouse over a SmartIcon. If you do not see the description appear, you may need to turn this feature on. Here's how to turn on the SmartIcon descriptions:

1. From your workspace, open the File and click Tools and SmartIcons. The SmartIcons dialog box appears, as shown in Figure 3.5.
2. Under Show, select Descriptions.
3. Click OK.

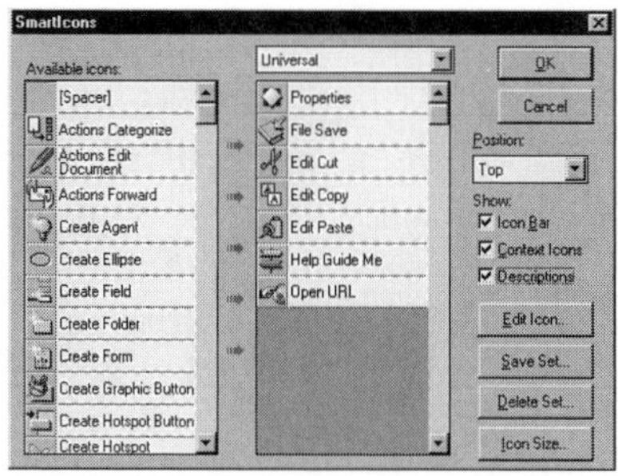

FIGURE 3.5 The SmartIcon dialog box.

To find out the purpose of each SmartIcon, place your cursor on the SmartIcon and a bubble appears listing the description of the SmartIcon (see Figure 3.6).

You can change the default SmartIcon set (called the Universal Set), by customizing it for your needs. For example, you might find it convenient to have the Print icon on your toolbar. To add or remove the Print icon:

1. From your workspace, open the File menu and choose Tools and SmartIcons from the menu.
2. The SmartIcon dialog box appears, as shown in Figure 3.7. The left panel shows available icons; the right panel shows icons that are currently selected for your "Universal Set" (the set in use). Scroll through the left panel of available icons until you locate the Printer icon.
3. Drag the Printer icon from the left panel to the right panel. Position it on the right panel in the exact position

you want it to appear on your toolbar. For example, placing this icon first on the list will result in it appearing first (on the far left) on the toolbar.

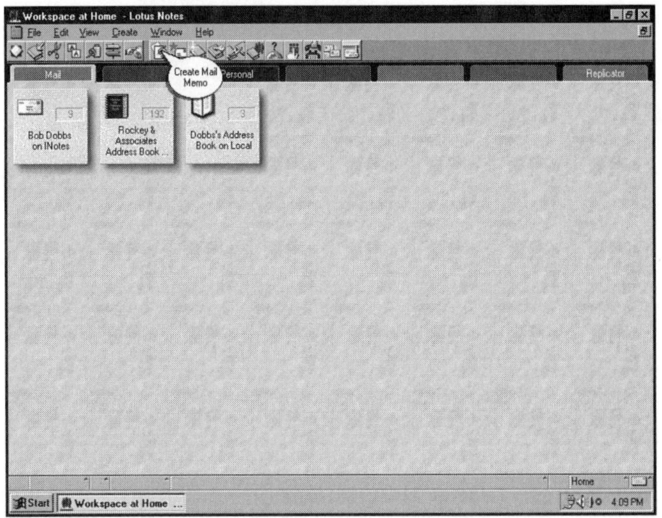

FIGURE 3.6 SmartIcon descriptions.

4. This causes the icons to move down in the list so that your Printer icon is first on the list.
5. (Optional) To remove a SmartIcon from the toolbar, select it from the icons in the right panel and drag it to the left panel.
6. Click OK to save your changes and close the window. The Printer icon appears on the toolbar.

You can also change the size of your SmartIcons. To do so:

1. From your workspace, open the File menu; choose Tools, SmartIcons from the menu.
2. The SmartIcon dialog box appears (see Figure 3.7). Click the Icon Size button. The Icon Size dialog box appears (see Figure 3.8).

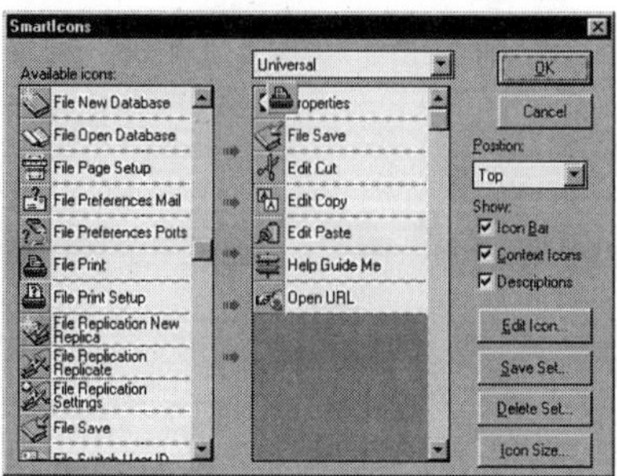

FIGURE 3.7 Customizing the SmartIcon set.

3. The default size for icons is small. Select large to change the icon size.
4. Click OK to close the Icon Size dialog box.
5. Click OK in the SmartIcon dialog box to save your changes and close the window.

You may want to change the position of your SmartIcon palette. The default position for your SmartIcon set is at the top of the screen. You can select Left, Right, Top, Bottom, or Floating.

Floating Palette A palette that appears in its own window rather than being anchored on the edge of the screen (as in Right, Left, Top, or Bottom). You can move the floating window around the screen by dragging its title bar; you can resize the window by dragging its borders.

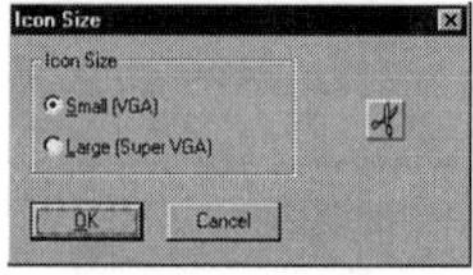

FIGURE 3.8 The Icon Size dialog box.

To change the position of your SmartIcon set:

1. From your workspace, open the File menu, and click Tools, SmartIcons from the menu.
2. The SmartIcon dialog box appears (see Figure 3.7). Click the Position drop-down menu. Select the position you want for your SmartIcon set.
3. Click OK in the SmartIcon dialog box to save your changes and close the window.
4. The SmartIcon set now appears in its new position (see Figure 3.9).

FIGURE 3.9 SmartIcon set with "Right" selected as position.

In this lesson, you learned about the standard elements of the Notes workspace and how to customize your workspace pages. You also worked with the database icons and SmartIcons. In the next lesson, you'll learn how to work in the Lotus Notes Mail database window.

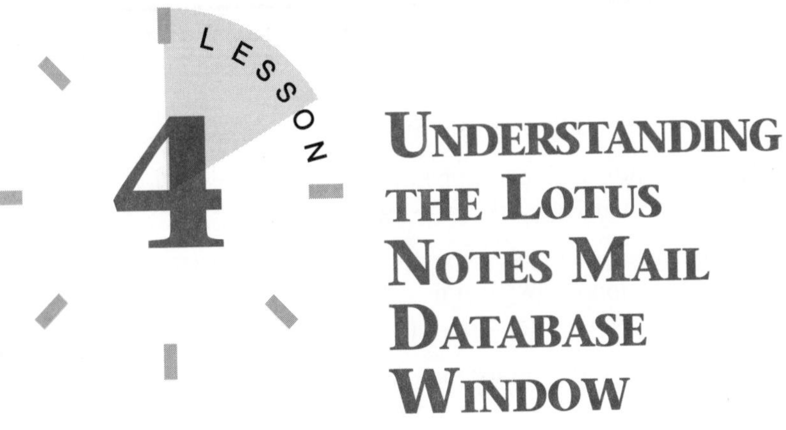

Understanding the Lotus Notes Mail Database Window

In this lesson, you learn how to open your Mail database, how to use views and folders, and how the Trash works.

Lotus Notes stores your mail in your Lotus Notes Mail database. The stored mail includes copies of messages you send. Your Mail workspace page contains an icon that represents the Mail database. This icon has a small picture of an envelope with your name on it.

To open the database, double-click the Mail Database icon.

Moving Around the Mail Database Window

When you open the Mail database, your screen is divided into two *panes* (see Figure 4.1). The *Navigator* pane is on the left. The Mail database has places in which you can store and view your messages. Use the Navigator pane to move to these different locations.

As you select different Navigator icons on the left pane of your screen, the documents that appear on the right side of your screen, in the *View* pane, will change. For example, if you select the Inbox icon on the left, you will see the contents of your Inbox listed like a table of contents on the right. The Inbox view (on the right) shows you who sent the message, the date of the message, and a brief description of the contents of the message.

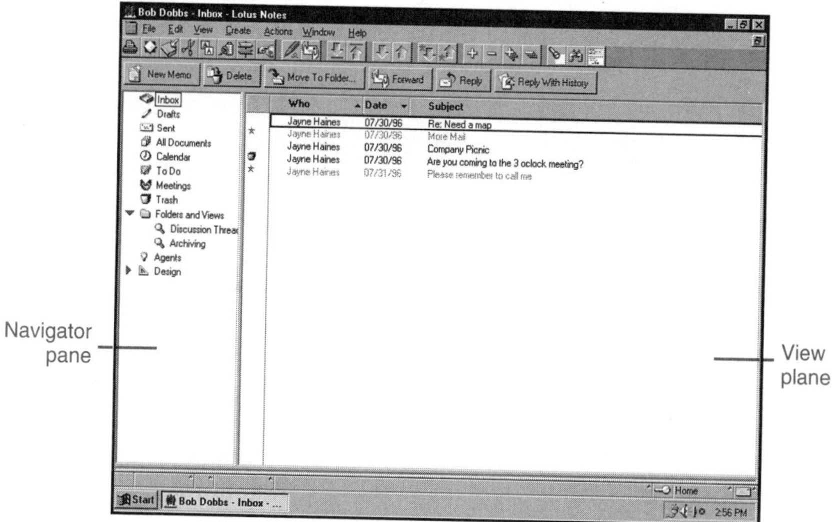

FIGURE 4.1 The Mail database window.

All the unread messages have a red star at the beginning of the line.

No Messages? If you're using Mail for the first time, you may not have any messages waiting. That will change quickly as you send mail messages to others and they reply back to you.

Resizing the Panes You can change the size of the Navigator and View panes to see more of one side or the other. Point to the line separating the two panes until your mouse pointer turns into a two-headed arrow separated by a black line. Then simply drag to the left or right.

Accessing Mail from the status bar (located at the bottom of the screen) indicates whether or not you're currently connected to your Domino server. A lightening bolt at the left of the status bar indicates that you are connected. No lightening bolt means that you are not currently connected to your server.

If you click the Mail icon on the right of the status bar, you see a pop-up menu (see Figure 4.2) that lets you choose common mail tasks:

- *Create Memo* starts a new mail message.
- *Scan Unread Mail* provides a list of the mail you haven't read.
- *Receive Mail* gets any new mail from the server.
- *Send Outgoing Mail* sends out any messages that you have written.
- *Send & Receive Mail* performs both actions at once.
- *Open Mail* opens the mail database.

To begin a task, select it from the pop-up menu. This pop-up menu is available in every window of Lotus Notes, so you can send and receive mail and perform other mail functions even when you're in another database or on the workspace itself.

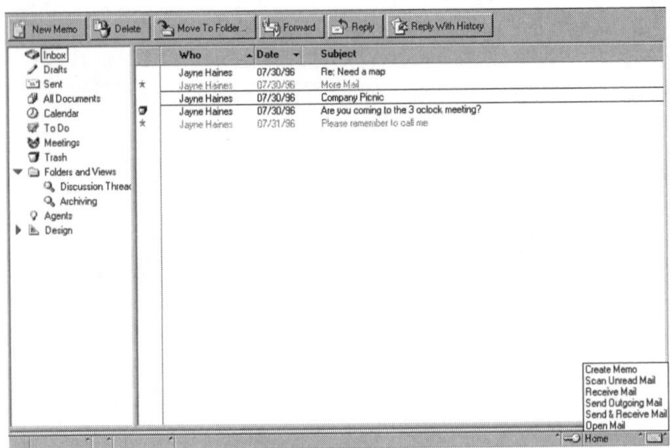

FIGURE 4.2 The Mail pop-up menu.

You can find the *Action bar* (see Figure 4.3) at the top of the Mail database window below the SmartIcons. The Action bar is context-sensitive and has several buttons on it. When you click one of the action buttons, it performs a program task such as saving your mail document.

Context-Sensitive The actions available to you depend on your current task or *context.* For example, if you are reading a document, one of the available actions would be to edit the document. But you couldn't save the document if you were just reading it, so the Save button would not appear. When you're editing a document, editing is no longer an available action (because you are *already* editing the document), but now you can *save* it.

When you select the Inbox, for example, there are six buttons on the action bar: *New Memo* creates a new piece of mail, *Delete* removes a message from the database, *Move to Folder* moves a document to a specific folder, *Forward* sends a copy of a message on to someone who did not receive the original, *Reply* for when you write a reply to a piece of mail, and *Reply with History* sends a copy of the original message along with your reply (more about these buttons in Lesson 11).

FIGURE 4.3 The Action bar of the Inbox.

USING FOLDERS AND VIEWS

The Navigator pane (see Figure 4.4) presents several folders and views for you to use when you work with your Mail documents.

In Lesson 1, you learned that a *view* is a *list* of documents, similar to a table of contents of the database. In the Mail database, a view lists your mail messages. There are different views that you can use to look at a list of mail messages sorted by date or by who sent them. Except for changing the way a view is sorted, you can't

FIGURE 4.4 The Navigator pane.

alter the contents of the view. But you can create your own folders and determine which messages you want to store in those folders. (In Lesson 13, you'll learn how to create folders.)

The Navigator pane has a series of pre-manufactured views and folders. The first icon on the Navigator is the *Inbox*. When you click the Inbox icon, you can see a list of all of the messages you have received. Those messages stay there until you move them to another folder or delete them. The Inbox is the default view when you open the Mail database for the first time. From then on, whatever view you have open when you close your Mail database is the view you will see the next time you open it.

There are times that you begin to write a message and decide not to send it right away. Maybe you need to add information to it. Perhaps you're being called away from your desk. You can save a message without sending it. The message will be stored in *Drafts*. When you want to go back to the message and finish it, click the Drafts icon in the Navigator pane to see a list of your drafts. To finish your draft, select and open the document, finish your work, and send the message.

Mail stores messages you send in Sent unless you move or delete them. To check the messages you have already sent, click the Sent icon.

All Documents displays all the messages that are currently in your Mail database.

Calendar allows you to make appointments on your personal calendar and to make appointments with others who use Notes Mail on your server. You'll learn more about calendars in Lesson 19.

And what would the well-organized person be without a *To Do* list? You can use Lotus Notes Mail to assign tasks to other people as well as to yourself. When you click the To Do icon, you will see a list of these tasks. The View pane lists a description of each task, the due date, and the person assigned to do the task. You'll work extensively with tasks in Lesson 17.

Meetings is a list of your appointments sorted by date, time and subject.

Documents that you mark for deletion are stored in Trash.

Folders and views contains two default views: Discussion Thread and Archiving. Use the Discussion Thread view to see messages grouped with their replies so you can follow an entire conversation. The Archiving view lists the documents you *archived* from this database. You archive messages to save space in your Mail database by creating a new database and sending your old and expired messages to that database.

Agents are like macros. They automate tasks such as managing documents, manipulating fields, and importing information from other applications. They are beyond the scope of this book.

Design allows you to design Notes databases, views, and forms. This also is beyond the scope of this book.

Where Are Those Views? If you can't see the Discussion Thread and Archiving views listed in the Navigator, check the little triangle in front of Folders and Views. This triangle is called a *twistee.* Is it pointing down or to the right? If it is pointing right, click the twistee triangle and it will turn down. Now you should see those views.

What Is a Default? A predefined system setting that you can chose to override. For example, the default font for Lotus Notes Mail is Helvetica, but you can change it to another font.

USING THE ALL DOCUMENTS VIEW

When you have mail in your mailbox, you'll appreciate these different views. If you don't have any mail yet, don't panic. It's still a good exercise to click through these views. By the time you start receiving mail, you'll have a good grasp on moving around the Mail database.

When you click the All Documents icon in the Navigator pane, you can see all of the documents currently in your Mail database displayed in the View pane—both the ones you sent and the ones you received (see Figure 4.5). For each document, you can see who sent it, the date it was sent, and the subject of the message.

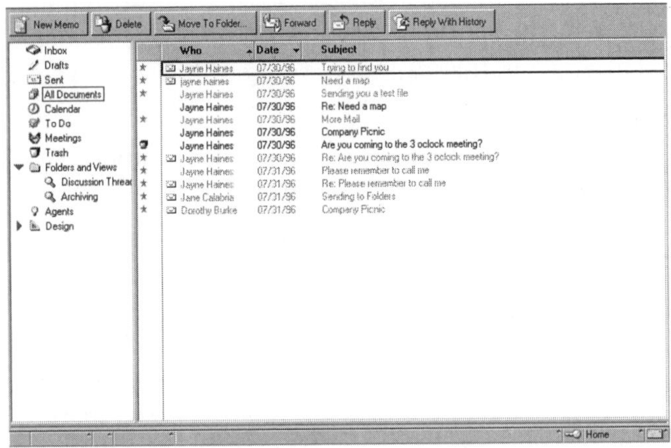

FIGURE 4.5 The All Documents view.

You can sort the documents by the name of the person (who) or by the date. However, you can't sort all views. How can you tell whether you can sort a view? The column headers have little triangles on them. The Who column header has an up triangle that indicates that this column will sort in *ascending* order (alphabetically A to Z). The Date column has a down triangle, which means this column will sort in *descending* order (most recent to oldest).

To resort the columns, click the appropriate column header button to change the order (you don't have to click right on the triangle). Clicking the Who column header sorts the documents alphabetically; clicking the Date column header sorts the documents in date order. You don't have the option to sort it both ways (by who, then by date) at the same time in this view. If the option to sort both ways were available in this view, the triangles would point both up and down on the column header. You might see that type of sort option in other databases.

If you connect to the server at work, your mail may not appear in your view as quickly as it arrives in your mailbox. Lotus Notes can notify you with a beeping sound or with a message on the screen that says you have new mail. Lesson 20 describes how to set the options for mail notification.

To refresh your view and see the new mail listed, click the Refresh icon in the upper left corner of the View pane or press F9. The refresh icon can appear in any view of Lotus Notes if a document has been added or modified during the time you have the view open. Use the F9 key to refresh a view when you see the refresh icon.

UNDERSTANDING TRASH

As you view your messages, you can mark the ones you don't want by selecting the message and then clicking the Delete button in the action bar or by pressing the Delete key on your keyboard. A Trashcan icon appears in the document row. When you leave the database, Mail displays a message asking if you want to delete the marked items. You can select Yes or No.

If you choose No, Mail removes the Trashcan icon and your message remains in its location.

If you choose Yes, your messages will be deleted from the database. If you choose No, your messages go right into the *Trash,* although you can still see them in the All Documents view (they'll have a Trashcan icon in front of the document row). You can decide later if you want to keep them or not. After all, you wouldn't be the first person to go through your trash to find something you shouldn't have thrown out.

When you click the Trash icon (see Figure 4.6), you can select a document and pull it out of the Trash by clicking the Remove from Trash Action bar button. You can also empty your Trash, hopefully, without being reminded. Emptying your Trash will permanently remove all the documents listed there from the database, so be very sure you want to do this before you click the Empty Trash Action bar button.

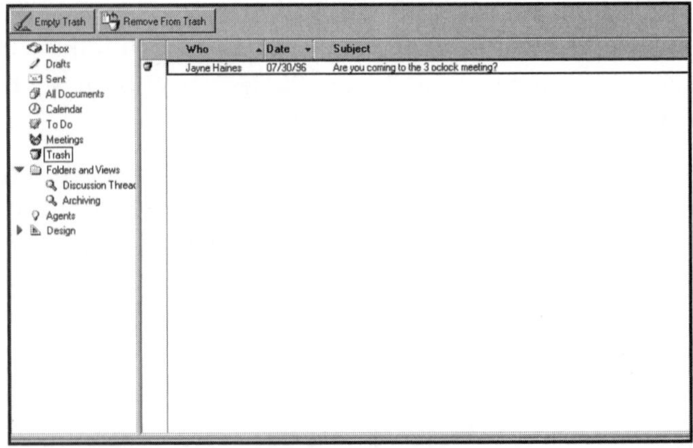

FIGURE 4.6 The Trash view.

In this lesson, you learned about opening your Mail database, using the different views and folders, and how to use Trash. In the next lesson, you learn about using Lotus Notes Help.

Lesson 5
Using Lotus Notes Help

In this lesson, you learn how to use Lotus Notes Help. You also learn how to perform searches within the Help database.

Understanding Lotus Notes Help

Help, like all information stored in Lotus Notes, is a database. That fact may not be obvious to you since you can access Help in so many ways. In other Lotus Notes databases, the only way to access the information contained in the database is to open the database. With Help, you don't have to double-click the database icon because you can also access it from the Help menu.

Lotus Notes has two versions of Help: Notes Help and Notes Help Lite.

> *Notes Help* is a larger database complete with navigators and is usually stored on the Domino server. Help is accessible to users who are constantly connected to the server.
>
> *Notes Help Lite* is the database used for desktops or laptops that have minimal disk space available and whose operator might need to access Help when not connected to the Domino server. In Help Lite, you'll find the most frequently used Help topics. If you're using the Help Lite database, you'll have less information available. You'll also have fewer views available. For instance, you won't have the option for the "Visual Index" view, discussed later in this lesson.

If you aren't sure which version you have, Help or Help Lite, look for the Help database icon on your workspace (see Figure 5.1). The database title indicates which version you have. If the database icon says Help, you have the larger Help database. If the database icon says Help Lite, you have the smaller of the Help databases installed.

FIGURE 5.1 The Notes Help and Notes Help Lite database icons.

If you don't see a Help database icon on your workspace, you can add it by opening the File menu and selecting Database, Open. Select Notes Help or Notes Help Lite from the database list on the server.

No Help icon? Be aware that if you're connected to a Notes server, you don't really need the Help database icon. Help is still available to you through the Help menu.

After you add the database icon to your workspace, you can access the Help database by double-clicking its icon or by opening the Help menu. Opening the Help menu is the method used for most Windows-based software.

You move around and find information in the Help database the same way you move around and find information in other Lotus Notes databases, through views and searches. But as previously said, you can get to the information in the database in one of several ways:

- You can use the menu (Help, Help Topics), and you'll see the Help database table of contents.
- You can press the F1 key, and you'll see a list of hypertext options that help you answer the question "What do you want to do?"
- You can use the Guide Me option for accessing context-sensitive Help.

USING THE HELP MENU

Take a look at how to use the menu to access Help. From your workspace, open the Help menu and select Help Topics. You'll see the main view of the Help database called the Index view. The Index view is the default view; this view displays the contents of the entire database (see Figure 5.2).

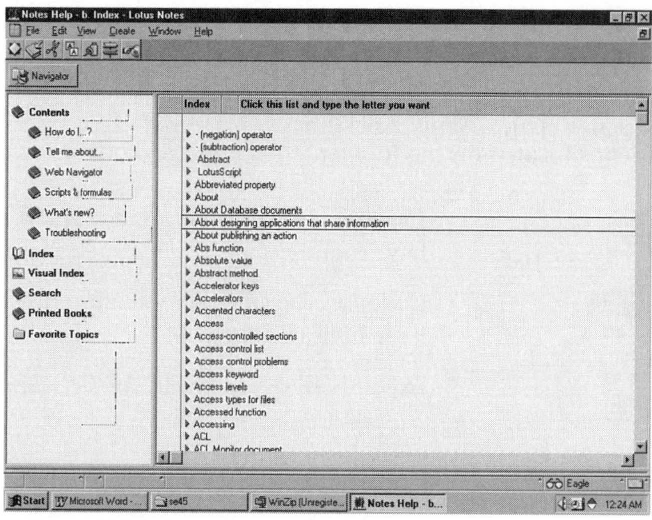

FIGURE 5.2 The Help database Index view.

This view takes advantage of collapsed (see Figure 5.3) and expanded (see Figure 5.4) views. Notice the little triangles that appear in front of some of the view topics? If the triangle is pointing to the right, this means that the line of text you see is a *category*. A category is not an actual document; it is a *categorization* of the documents listed beneath it. To see the documents beneath a category, click the triangle. The triangle will now point down and the documents appear beneath the category (see Figure 5.4).

To read a Help topic, simply double-click the document you want to read. Press Esc to return to the Index view.

▶ Assigning mail tasks

FIGURE 5.3 A Help Topic category (collapsed view).

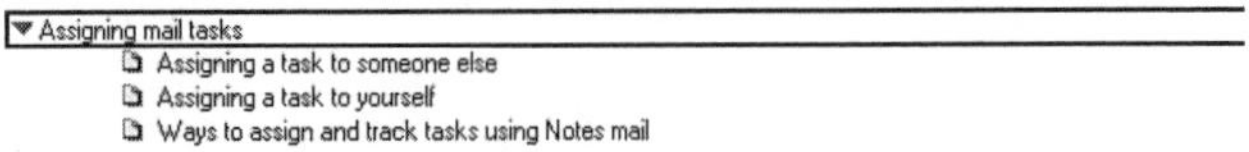

▼ Assigning mail tasks
Assigning a task to someone else
Assigning a task to yourself
Ways to assign and track tasks using Notes mail

FIGURE 5.4 A Help Topic category (expanded view).

When the triangle points down, this is an *expanded* view. One way of expanding and collapsing views is to click the triangle. If the category is collapsed, clicking will expand it. If the category is expanded, clicking will collapse it. You can also use the SmartIcons located on the toolbar to expand and collapse views.

Expands the category you currently have highlighted.

Collapses the category you currently have highlighted.

Expands all categories in the database.

Collapses all categories in the database.

In the left panel of the Index view are navigators to other available views (see Figure 5.5).

Here's a quick summary of what these Help views provide:

- **How do I . . . ?** Contains a list of task-oriented functions such as Ways to address mail.
- **Tell me about . . .** Provides shortcuts, notes, database design, and management concepts.
- **Web Navigator** Contains Help information on the Navigator.

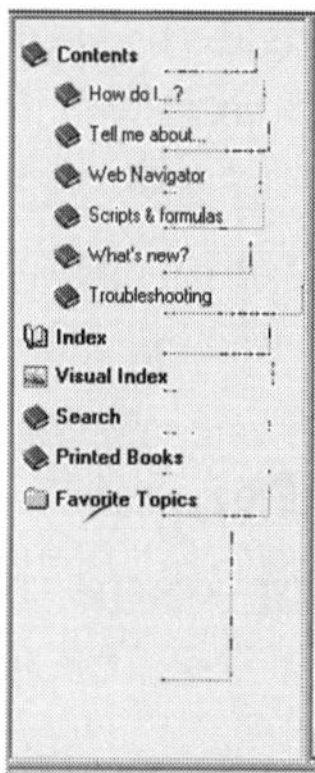

FIGURE 5.5 The Help database Index view navigators.

- **Scripts and Formulas** Contains information on LotusScript and formulas.
- **What's new?** Contains information about Lotus Notes Release 4 for users of previous versions.
- **Troubleshooting** Lists and answers common questions and meanings of error messages.
- **Index** Displays a list of categorized Help topics. This is the default view for the database.
- **Visual Index** Graphically displays Help topics. This feature is only available in the Help version of Notes Help, not in the Help Lite version.
- **Search** Lists topics alphabetically, without categories.
- **Printed Books** Contains Notes documentation in book form, such as the Programmers Guide and User Guide.

As you select a view navigator on the *left* of your screen, the contents will change on the *right* of your screen. Each time you change views, you can navigate to another view or press the Esc key to return to your workspace. Take a minute and try some of the navigators.

You can disable the navigator by clicking the Navigator button on the Action bar. This will take you to the Folders view.

USING THE VISUAL INDEX

The **Visual Index** view displays the contents of the database with navigators, as shown in Figure 5.6. You will have this view available only if you are using the Help version available on the Notes server. To see the Visual Index view:

1. Click the Visual Index navigator. The Visual Index view displays navigators on the left pane of your screen, representing topics (see Figure 5.6). Investigate the Workspace Management navigator.

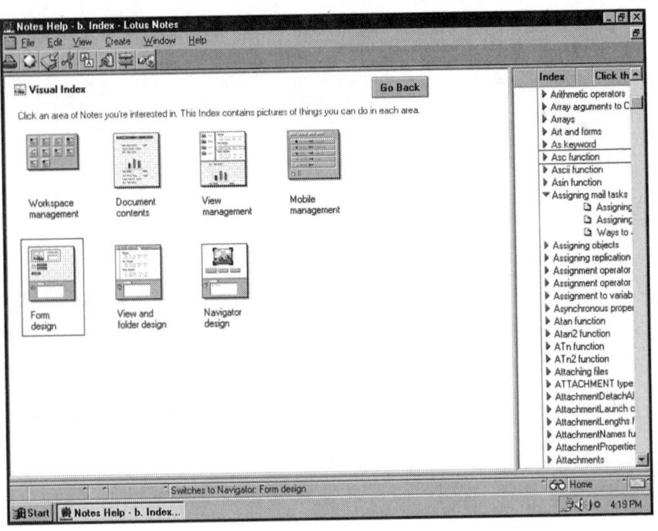

FIGURE 5.6 The Lotus Notes Help database Visual Index view.

2. Click the Workspace Management navigator.

3. A picture of the workspace appears. Tiny yellow bubbles act as *hotspots* to lead you to help on a given topic (see Figure 5.7).

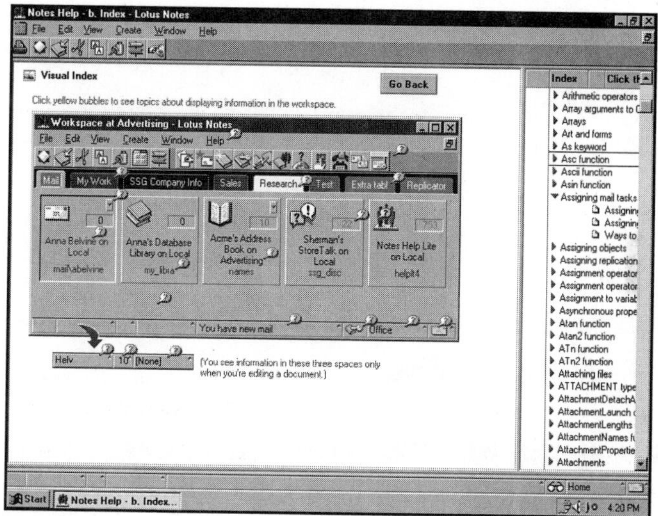

FIGURE 5.7 Tiny yellow bubbles act as hotspots for getting help.

4. Click on the tiny yellow bubble that points to the My Work tab in the picture of the workspace. The Entering a name on a Workspace tab Help topic appears (see Figure 5.8).

5. Click the Go Back button in the action bar to return to the Workspace navigator. Then click again to return to the Visual Index view and once again to return to the Index view.

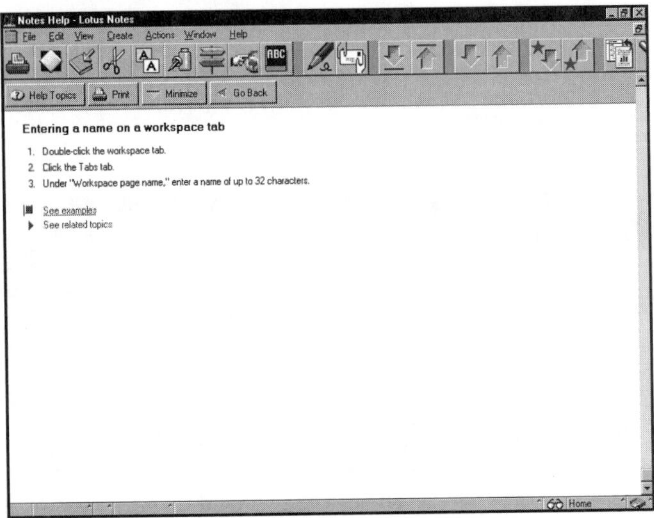

FIGURE 5.8 Click a bubble for help on that topic.

PERFORMING SEARCHES

There are two ways to search for information in the Help database: Quick Search and Guide Me. Quick Search searches through the titles of the Lotus Notes Help documents but not through the contents of the documents. Quick Search works only if your view is expanded. Instead of scrolling or using the Page Down key, you can use Quick Search to move quickly through the database screens. For example, if you want to find information on printing from the Index view, you need only to press the letter P on your keyboard. The Quick Search dialog box appears, as shown in Figure 5.9.

FIGURE 5.9 Quick Search dialog box.

After the dialog box appears, you can type the first letter of a word, the first part of a word, or the entire word you want to search for. If you type only the letter P and click OK, the first document title that starts with the letter P displays highlighted. If you type the entire word Print, the search will find the first document title that starts with the word Print.

Another way to search a database is to search the database document contents for words not included in the title of the document. The Help database has a Search view for that purpose. You can use this view to search for a specific word or phrase. You can access the Search view by clicking the Search navigator located in the Main, or Index view. To use the Search view and search for a word or phrase in the Help database:

1. Click the Search navigator.
2. Click the Show Search Bar button on the Action bar. The Search bar is under the toolbar, as shown in Figure 5.10.

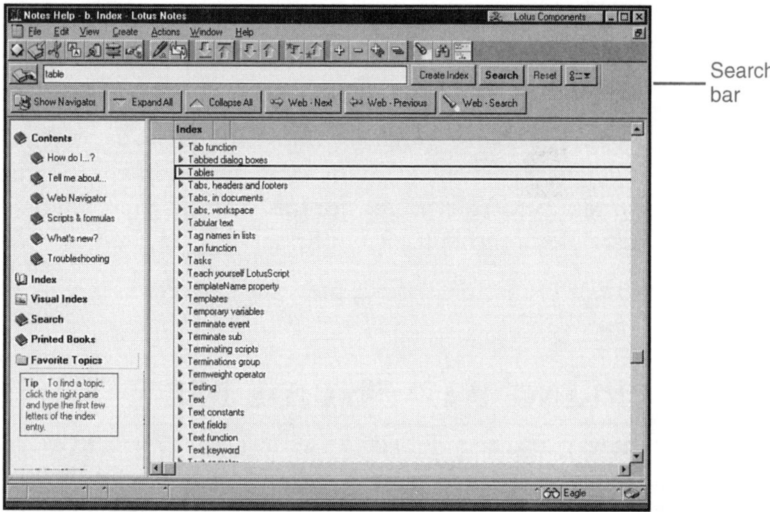

FIGURE 5.10 The Lotus Notes Search bar.

Search Bar A set of tools that help you find information in Lotus Notes databases. You can use the Search bar in most of your databases in Lotus Notes. You should have your views expanded to search all documents in the database.

3. Click the text box of the Search bar.
4. Type the word or phrase you want to search for; type **mail**.
5. Click the Search button.
6. The search results will appear in the right pane of the Help window. To access any of the search results documents, simply double-click the document in the right pane of your screen.
7. Notice that the number of documents found that meet your search criteria is indicated on the status bar.
8. To return to the Index view of Help, click the Index navigator.
9. To refresh your screen, click the Reset button located on the Action bar. The word mail will remain in your Search bar text box. You can replace this the next time you do a search for another topic or phrase.
10. To exit the Help database, press the Esc key.

WORKING WITH GUIDE ME

Another way to access Help is to use the context-sensitive *Guide Me* feature of Lotus Notes. To activate Guide Me, press the F1 key. When you use this key, instead of showing you the views just discussed, Lotus Notes displays a list of topics asking you What do you want to do? followed by topics that you can double-click to search out how to perform tasks. You can use this at any time from any place while working in Lotus Notes.

1. Click the Inbox navigator of your Lotus Notes Mail database.
2. Press the key for help.
3. A screen appears asking What do you want to do?. Double-click Print.

   A list of print topics appears.
4. Double-click Print one document?.
5. Now you can read the instructions for printing a document. To exit this screen and the Mail database, press the Esc key until you return to your workspace.

Getting Additional Help for Mobile Users

If you're a mobile user or responsible for helping mobile users, you may want to access the Notes Mobile Survival Kit. This database contains troubleshooting tips and general information on modems, remote Notes, and wireless issues. The Notes Mobile Survival Kit has the latest modem command files, pager files, and script files. It also contains presupport call questions that you should check out before you call for technical support.

The Notes Mobile Survival Kit (Mod_Surv.Nsf) may be stored on your Lotus Notes server. Check with your Notes administrator to get help in accessing or replicating this database.

In this lesson, you learned how to access and use Lotus Notes Help and how to search for information in the Help database. In the next lesson, you'll learn how to create mail messages.

LESSON

6

Creating Mail

In this lesson, you learn how to create and address a mail message.

You can start a mail message from several places in Lotus Notes.

- If you are on the workspace, choose Create, Mail, Memo or click the Create Mail Memo SmartIcon.
- If you are on the workspace and you have selected your Mail database icon, choose Create, Memo.
- If you have opened the Mail database and can see the Action bar, click the New Memo button.
- Click the Mail icon on the status bar and choose Create Memo.

Using the Address Options

When the New Memo window opens, you see several *fields* that you must complete (see Figure 6.1). A field holds a piece of information stored in the database. Square brackets mark the fields where you enter text.

Entering text in Lotus Notes fields is like typing in a word processor. You can use the Backspace and Delete keys to remove unwanted text. You can move the insertion point (cursor) using the arrow keys or by clicking with the mouse. You can insert text wherever you place the cursor.

The first field to complete on your memo is the To field. This is where you put the name of the person who will receive your message. You can enter this information by using the Typeahead option or by looking up names in the address books.

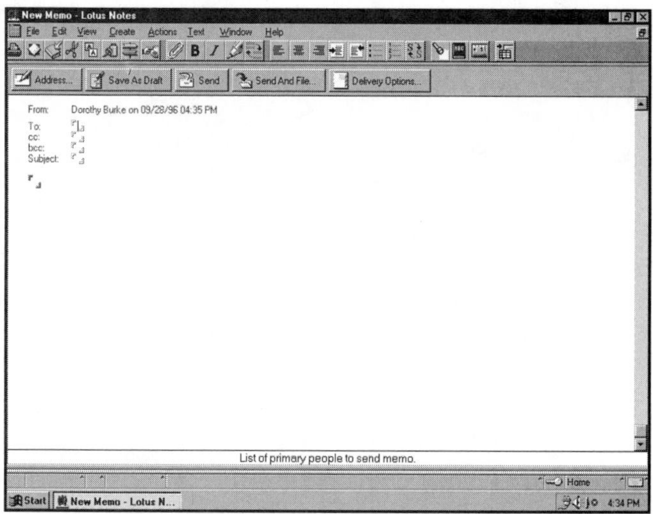

FIGURE 6.1 A new mail memo.

USING THE TYPEAHEAD OPTION

The *Typeahead* option saves you work. When you type the first letter of a name in the To field, Typeahead finds and enters the full name of the first person in your address book that starts with that letter. For example, when you type **P**, Notes fills in the name Paul Abbott. Then as you enter the second letter, **e**, Notes finds and enters Peter Anderson, and so on.

Typeahead will also accept last names. When you enter the beginning letter(s) of the last name and press Tab to go to the next field, Notes finds the name and reverses the order when it fills in the field. So, when you type **A**, Notes might find Ann Rutherford. But when you type a **b** and press Tab, Notes should locate the last name Abbott and insert Paul Abbott in the address field.

Typeahead only works if the name of the recipient is in an address book. Otherwise, you must type the full name and address of the person.

Address Book A database that contains all the names and electronic mail addresses of all the users you communicate with through e-mail. Lotus Notes Mail has two address books: Personal and Public. The Personal Address Book is stored on your local drive, while the Public Address Book is on the server. Lesson 8 covers the address books in detail.

If you want to address the memo to more than one person, separate the names with commas. Typeahead works for each name.

ADDRESSING FROM THE ADDRESS BOOK

If you aren't sure of a person's last name or the spelling of his name, you can look him up in the address book. You can choose to insert the person's name into the To, cc, or bcc fields.

In the cc (carbon copy) field, enter the names of people you want to receive the message you send to the recipient. The names in the cc field appear on the recipient's message, and all these people will also see the cc names.

Use the bcc (blind carbon copy) field to send hidden copy. The name of the bcc recipient does not appear on any other messages; only you and the person you bcc know he received a copy. If you put two names in the bcc field, those two people don't know that the other received the message. To use an address book, follow these steps:

1. Click the Address button on the Action toolbar.

   When the Mail Address dialog box appears, you'll see a list of names from your Personal Address Book (see Figure 6.2). At this point, your Personal Address Book is probably empty. To access the Public Address Book, click the drop-down menu and select Public Address Book. Remember, you must be able to attach to the server to access the Public Address Book.

2. Select the name of the person that you need from the available list of names. You can use the scrollbar to move up or down the list.

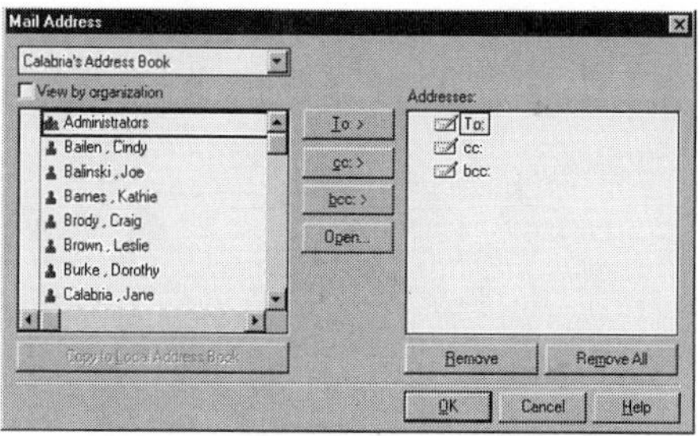

FIGURE 6.2 The Mail Address dialog box.

3. Click the To, cc, or bcc button, depending on which address field you want to fill.

4. Repeat the last two steps for each name you want to enter.

5. Click OK.

If you are sending Internet mail, refer to Lesson 8 to learn how to address Internet e-mail.

FILLING IN THE MAIL MESSAGE DOCUMENT

Complete the Subject field by entering a short description of your memo in this field, similar to a headline for a newspaper article. Every time someone replies to your message, her reply memo will show the same subject, which appears on all replies and replies to replies.

After the subject field is the body field. When you finish typing your message, you should spell check the message before you mail it. If you feel you don't need to spell check the message, click the Send button on the Action bar to send your mail (see Figure 6.3).

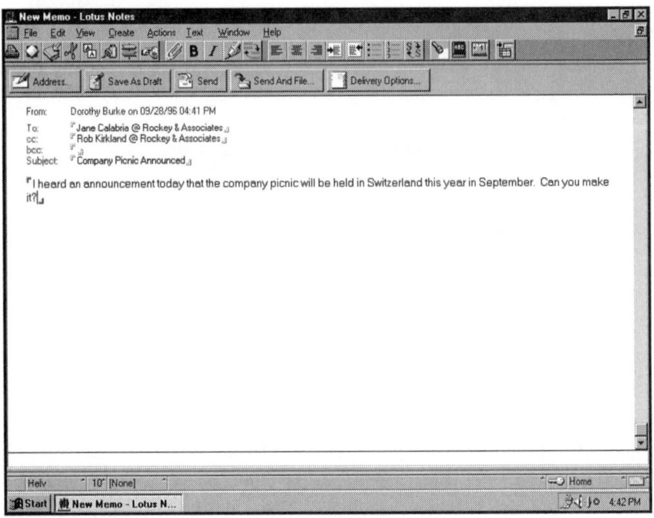

FIGURE 6.3 A completed mail message, ready to send.

USING SPELL CHECK

Spell Check compares your text against a stored spelling dictionary of tens of thousands of words. If any of your words aren't in the spelling dictionary, Spell Check alerts you that the word is possibly misspelled. In addition to your misspellings and typos, Spell Check will also alert you about proper names and unusual words that may be spelled correctly but are not in the spelling dictionary.

Running Spell Check doesn't guarantee a perfect mail message. If you accidentally type the word "form" when you wanted to type "from," Spell Check won't catch it. An incorrectly typed word may be a word found in the dictionary. Spell Check won't catch incorrect punctuation or missing words.

Lotus Notes looks in two dictionaries for correctly spelled words. The *main dictionary* is extensive, covering most of the common words in American English. Proper names, acronyms, and business jargon not included in the main dictionary, are then looked for in your *user dictionary*. The user dictionary is one you can add to.

Spell Check will also report duplicate words, such as "the the," but it won't look at single-character words such as "a" and "I" or words that are longer than 64 letters. It also ignores text that doesn't have any letters, such as the number 1,200,543.

When you want to check the spelling in your message, you must be in edit mode. Edit mode means that you have the ability to change the text in the document in which you are currently working. When you're *creating* a new mail message, you're automatically in edit mode.

To run Spell Check:

1. Choose Edit, Check Spelling or click the Edit Check Spelling SmartIcon. The Spell Check dialog box appears, as shown in Figure 6.4.

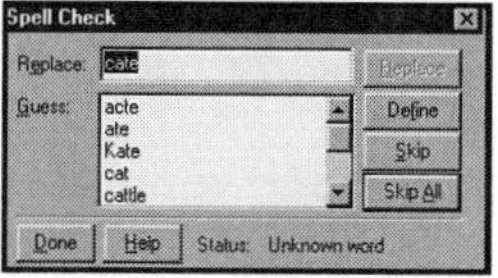

FIGURE 6.4 The Spell Check dialog box.

2. When Spell Check finds a word it doesn't recognize, choose one of the following options:

   Skip Ignores the misspelling and goes on to the next word. Use this option when the word is spelled correctly.

   Skip All Tells Notes to ignore all the instances of this word in the message. This is useful when a correctly spelled proper name crops up several times in a memo.

   Define Lets you add the word to your user dictionary. Once added, Spell Check will see this word as a correctly spelled word.

   Replace Lets you change an incorrect spelling to a correct one. If the correct spelling of the word shows up in the Guess box, click the correct guess and then the

Replace button. If Spell Check provides no suggestions and you know the correct spelling, click in the Replace box and make the correction by deleting or adding characters. Then click Replace to make the change in your message.

3. Once the Spell Check ends, click Done.

No Spell Check Icon? If you don't see the Spell Check SmartIcon on your toolbar, refer to Lesson 3 to add it to your toolbar.

By default, Spell Check checks your entire mail message. If you want to Spell Check one word or a paragraph, select the word or text with your mouse; then start the Spell Check as previously mentioned.

To change words that you add to your user dictionary:

1. Choose File, Tools, User Preferences. In the User Preferences dialog box, click the User Dictionary button (see Figure 6.5).

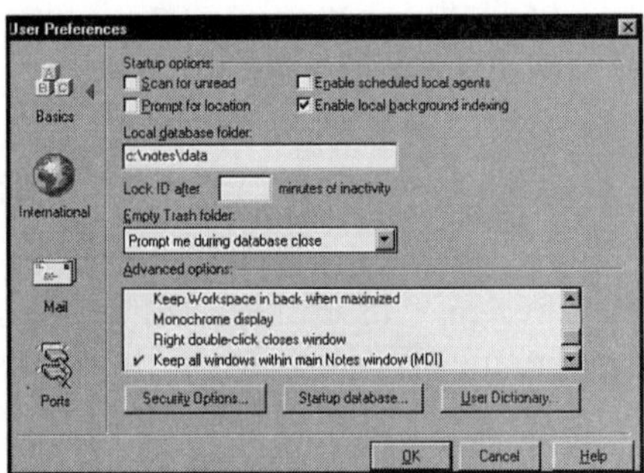

FIGURE 6.5 The User Preferences dialog box.

2. You can then make any of the following changes:

   - To delete the incorrectly spelled word, select it and click Delete.
   - To change a misspelled word, select it from the list, enter the correct spelling in the small text box at the bottom of the dialog box, and then click Update.
   - To add a word, enter it in the small text box and click Add.

3. When you finish, click OK.

In this lesson, you learned how to fill out a mail message and use the Typeahead option. In the next lesson, you learn how to format text.

Formatting Text

In this lesson, you learn about rich text fields how to format text, and how to add special characters in your mail messages.

Understanding Rich Text Fields

Until now, most of the fields you've been working with have been *text* fields. In a text field, you can enter text or numbers, but you can't format the text. To format text is to make your text bold, italic, and underlined. You can also change the font and the font size.

The body field of the mail memo is a different kind of text field; it's a *rich text field*. You can also add graphics, attachments, objects, hotspots, pop-ups, special characters, and tables to this field.

No Size Limit A rich text field has virtually no size limit. However, if your message is longer than one screen, consider typing your message in a word processing program. You can then attach this file to your Mail message.

You can identify a rich text field by looking at the Lotus Notes status bar. When your cursor is in a rich text field, the font name, font size, and paragraph style assigned to that field appear on the status bar. Additionally, red square brackets surround the field. Figure 7.1 shows the Mail Memo form with the cursor in the To field, which is a text field, but not a rich text field. No formatting information appears in the status bar.

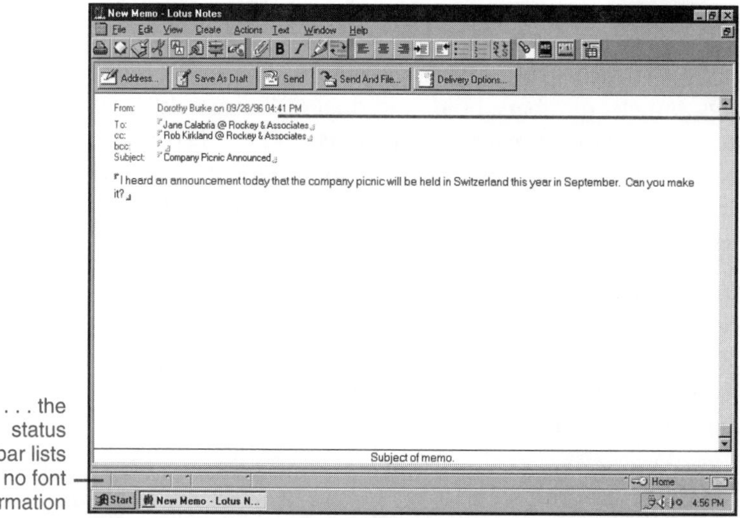

FIGURE 7.1 The status bar indicates a text field.

Figure 7.2 shows the cursor positioned in the body field, which is a rich text field. The status bar displays information about the font name, font size, and paragraph style.

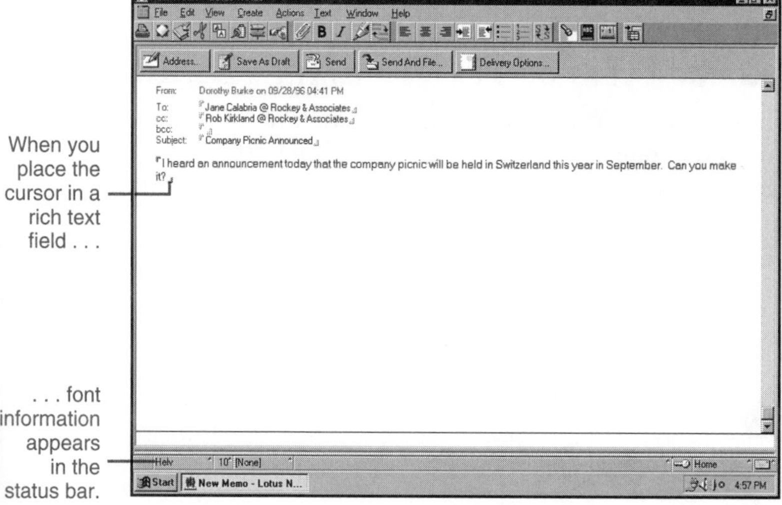

FIGURE 7.2 The status bar indicates a rich text field.

METHODS OF FORMATTING TEXT

To change your text's appearance, you can add headings, subheadings, bullets, numbers, bold, and italics. You can also underline your text, change the fonts and colors, and use strikethrough, superscript, and subscript. You can also use these formatting options in combination, such as ***bold and italic***, or <u>**bold and underlined**</u>, or <u>*italic and underlined.*</u>

You can format text using two methods. With the first method, type your text and then use your mouse or keystrokes to select the text you want to format. After you select the text, apply your formatting options. With the second method, you select the formatting options first and then type the text.

Selecting Text Place your mouse pointer to the left of the word(s) you want to select, hold down the left mouse button, and drag the mouse across the words. Release the mouse when the word(s) you want selected appear highlighted. To deselect the text, click anywhere in the window.

CHANGING TYPES OF TEXT FORMATS

Like most word processing programs, you can find text formatting options in the toolbar, the menu bar, or by using keystrokes. To change text formatting using buttons on the toolbar, follow these steps:

1. Place your cursor in the rich text field where you want the new formatting style to begin.

2. In the toolbar, click one of the following buttons:

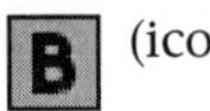

(icon 02) Bold

(icon 02) Italic

3. Begin typing your mail message.
4. To end formatting, click the toolbar button again.

Changing Existing Text To change existing text, select the text, then press one of the formatting buttons on the toolbar.

Lotus Notes also offers text formatting options through the Text Properties box.

Strikethrough Use this to show text that has been struck from a document, ~~such as this~~. Use Superscript to place text above the line, such as a trademark™ notation and Subscript to place text below the line, such as in the H_20 chemical symbol.

To change text formatting options using the Text Properties box, follow these steps:

1. Place the cursor in the area of the rich text field where you want to begin your new formatting style.

2. Click the Properties SmartIcon in the toolbar. The Text Properties box appears, as shown in Figure 7.3.
3. (Optional) If you don't see the word Text next to Properties for: in the title bar, click the drop-down list and choose Text.
4. In the Style: list, click the formatting style you want to apply. A check mark indicates that a style is active. You can choose more than one style. (Use the scrollbar on the right to locate styles that are not displayed.)
5. Click the Close (X) button in the upper right corner of the Properties box to apply the formatting style.
6. Begin typing text.

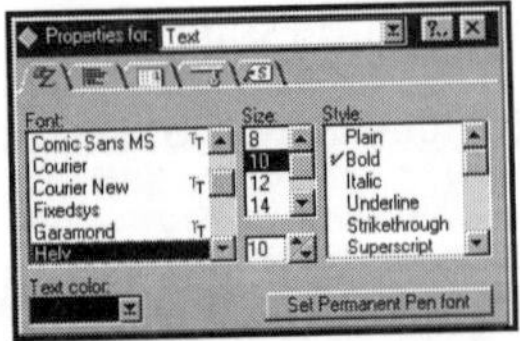

FIGURE 7.3 The Text Properties box.

Shortcut Another way to access the Properties box is to place your cursor in the rich text field and right-click. Select Text Properties from the pop-up menu.

FONTS AND SPECIAL CHARACTERS

The default font for the mail message body field is Helvetica, which appears on the status bar as Helv.

To change your font, click the Helv font button on the status bar and select a new font from the pop-up list (see Figure 7.4). You can also change your font through the Text Properties box. (The steps for accessing and selecting options from the Text Properties box were described earlier in this lesson.)

Be Conservative Lotus Notes supplies a large list of fonts, but don't use them all in the same mail message. Many available computer fonts are decorative and fine to use for a couple of words, but difficult to read in large blocks of text. Additionally, not everyone shares the fonts you have on your computer.

Sometimes, you might want to include *special characters* in the body of your mail message, which don't appear on your keyboard, such as a copyright mark ©. You can find these characters in the LMBCS (Lotus MultiByte Character Set) table. Table 7.1 shows a partial listing of special characters.

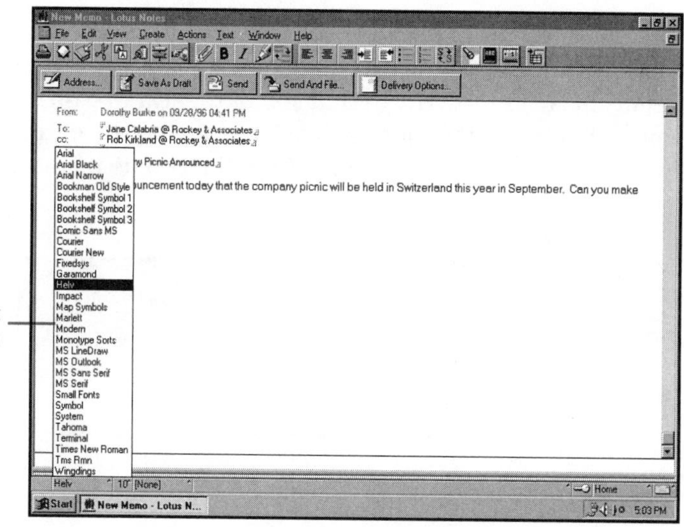

FIGURE 7.4 The font pop-up menu located on the status bar.

To enter any of these special characters into the body of your mail message, place your cursor at the insertion point where you want the character to appear, hold down the Alt key, and type the character sequence listed in Table 7.1.

TABLE 7.1 SPECIAL CHARACTERS

CHARACTER	TYPE THIS
£	L=
®	RO
1/2	12
1/4	14
©	CO
¢	c/
¥	Y=
°	^O

SIZE

Font size, or type size, is measured in points. A larger point number results in larger text. The default size of the text in Notes is 10 points. To change the font size, click the Size button on the status bar, and select one of the sizes from the pop-up menu (see Figure 7.5).

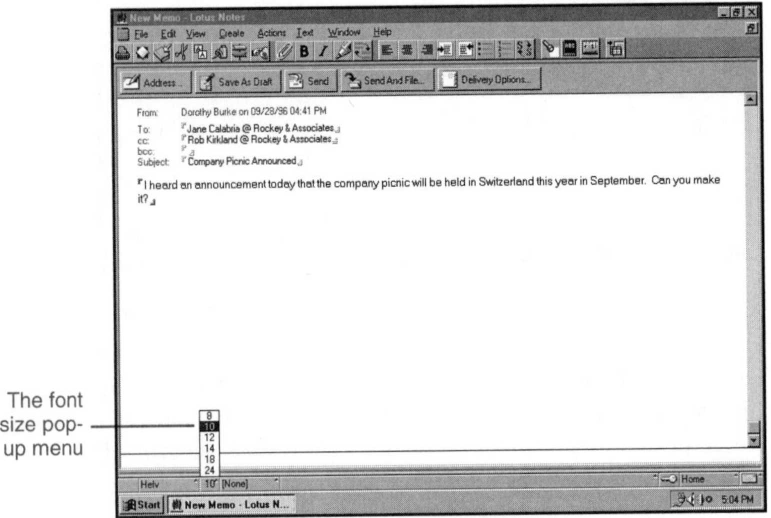

FIGURE 7.5 The font size pop-up menu located on the status bar.

If you want a size other than the ones listed in the pop-up menu, follow these steps:

1. Open the Properties dialog box and select Text from the drop-down list in the title bar. The Text tab appears (see Figure 7.3).
2. Click the up or down buttons below the Size list, to change to a nonstandard font size.

Closing the Properties Box You do not have to close the Properties box to apply formatting. Formatting options you select will take effect even with the Properties box open. You might want to leave the box open if you are performing several formatting options at one time. You can move the Properties box by dragging the title bar.

COLOR

One of the best ways to add emphasis and emotion to your text is with color. To add color to text, choose Text, Color from the menu bar, and then select a color name from the list. To see more color choices, click the Other button. The Properties box opens; you can choose a color from the Text color drop-down list by clicking the color swatch you want to apply to the text.

THE PERMANENT PEN

The *permanent pen* (a Lotus Notes term) allows you to add text in another color or font. This is especially useful for making comments that contrast with the regular text. Why would you use this instead of changing the text attributes the normal way? With the permanent pen, you don't have to change the text formatting every time you move the cursor.

To turn on the permanent pen, choose Text, Permanent Pen or click the Permanent Pen SmartIcon. Then type the text you want to appear in the permanent pen style. To stop the permanent pen style, click the Permanent Pen SmartIcon again.

To set the look of the permanent pen, open the Properties box and choose Text in the Properties for: field. Select the first tab (labeled AZ). Make all of your selections for the permanent pen; make sure you don't have any text selected before you do this. Click Set Permanent Pen font.

In this lesson, you learned about rich text fields and how to format text. You also learned how to insert special characters and apply the permanent pen. In the next lesson, you learn how to use the address books.

Lesson 8 Using the Address Books

In this lesson, you learn about the two address books found in Lotus Notes: the Public Address Book and the Personal Address Book.

Like mail, address books are databases. You store your e-mail addresses in Lotus Notes address books. In Lesson 6, you used the Public Address Book to add names to a mail memo. Lotus Notes has at least two address books available for your use, the Personal Address Book and the company or Public Address Book.

Your Personal Address Book has your name on it and is empty until you add people to it.

The Public Address Book contains the addresses of employees in your company who use Lotus Notes Mail. Your Lotus Notes administrator maintains this address book.

Using the Public Address Book

When your company or organization first sets up Lotus Notes, they establish a Public Address Book. The address of everyone in your company who uses e-mail and who you can access through Lotus Notes Mail is in that book. As new people come and other people leave, your administrator updates the information. You do not make entries in this book, although you may update your personal information, and you can use the other entries—very much like you use the public telephone book.

No Public Address Book icon? If you're a remote user, you may not see the Public Address Book icon. You can add it to your workspace as described in Lesson 24.

In addition to the employees listed in the Public Address Book, there may also be listings for people that your company contacts frequently via another Notes server or the Internet. These may be vendors, customers, information sources, or servers in other locations. If someone is listed in the Public Address Book, you should be able to send mail to them, no matter where they are located.

Your Notes administrator may have added address books from other companies to your server. If he has, you will be able to access multiple Public Address Books when you do address lookups. This is known as cascading address books.

To see the names listed in your Public Address Book, double-click the Public Address Book icon. In the Navigator pane (see Figure 8.1), click People to see a list of the people in the address book. To find out more information about an individual, double-click on that person's name. Press Esc to exit the person's document.

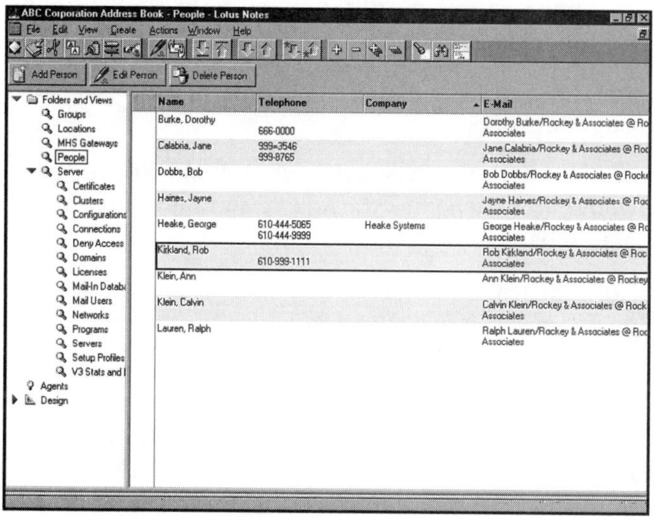

FIGURE 8.1 The Public Address Book.

USING YOUR PERSONAL ADDRESS BOOK

The Personal Address Book is where you store the names and addresses of all the people to whom you send e-mail and who are not included in the Public Address Book. Since everyone in your company is already in the Public Address Book, entries in your Personal Address Book are for people you want to send mail to through the Internet, or people who work for another company whose Lotus Notes server exchanges mail with your Lotus Notes server.

To open your Personal Address Book, double-click the database icon.

The Navigator pane provides views for companies, groups, locations, people, and the server.

Click People. The View pane shows you a list of all the people you have in your Personal Address Book, their telephone numbers, company names, and e-mail addresses. If you are new to Lotus Notes Mail, your address book is probably empty.

The information you store about a person—their e-mail address, company, and such—appears in a *Person document form*. Figure 8.2 shows a Person document.

To create a person document from the People view of your Personal Address Book:

1. Double-click your Personal Address Book icon on the workspace. Then click the Add Person button on the Action bar.
2. Choose Create, Person from the menu. The Person document appears (see Figure 8.2).
3. In the Name area, complete each field in the Person document by clicking within the square brackets and typing the appropriate information. Use the Tab key to move from field to field. For addressing purposes, the first

name and middle initial are optional but the last name is required.

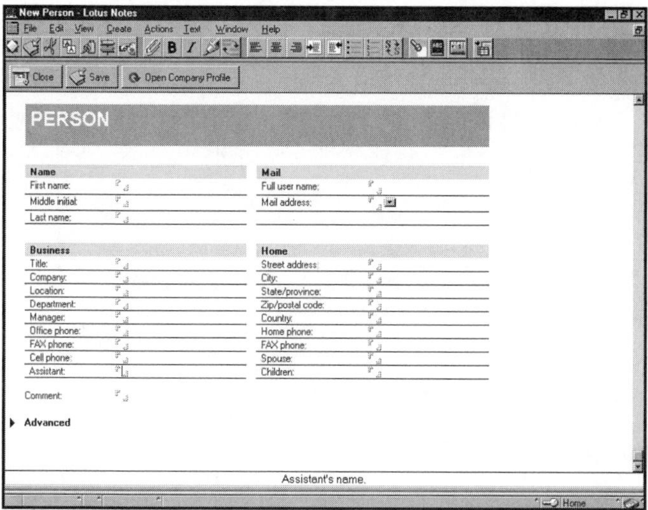

FIGURE 8.2 A Person document.

4. In the Mail area, type the person's full name in the Full user name field. This is the field that Lotus Notes uses in the Typeahead feature discussed in Lesson 6. It's important to fill in the information in this field correctly.
5. Click the down arrow key next to the field and the Mail Address Assistant dialog box appears (see Figure 8.3). In this dialog box, enter the type of mail system that person uses. Click OK.

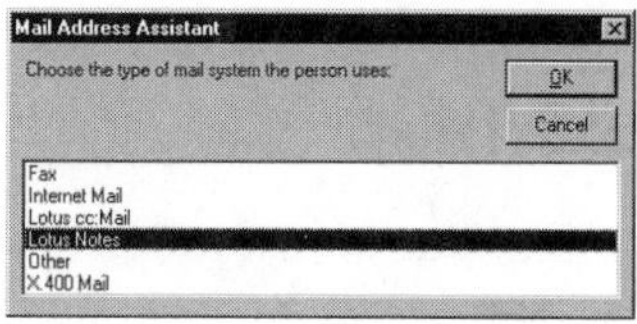

FIGURE 8.3 The first Mail Address Assistant dialog box.

6. A second Mail Address Assistant dialog box appears, which allows you to fill in the name and the address, or domain, of that user (see Figure 8.4). Fill in this information, and click OK.

What's a Domain? A Domain is a group of servers that share and are listed in one Public Address Book. If you don't know the domain name, see your Notes administrator.

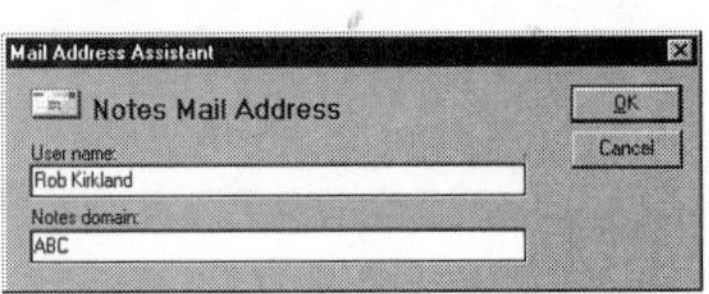

FIGURE 8.4 The second Mail Address Assistant dialog box.

7. Complete the information in the Business and Home areas of the document. These fields are not mandatory, but this is a useful central storage place for information.
8. Click the Save button on the Action bar to save this information in your address book. Then click the Close button.

CREATING AND USING GROUPS

If you send an e-mail to more than one person, you can type each person's name separated by a comma, or you can create a *Group*. To create a group:

1. Open your Personal Address Book.
2. In the Navigator pane, select Group.
3. Click the Add Group button on the Action bar.

4. The Group dialog box appears (see Figure 8.5). Type a name for your group in the Group name field. Make the group name descriptive but short enough to type easily.

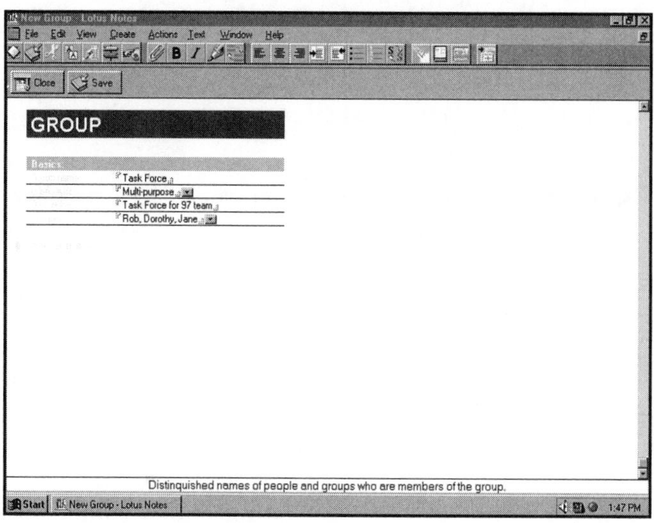

FIGURE 8.5 A Group document.

5. To fill out the Group type field, click the down arrow next to see a list of group types and choose one of the following:

   - Multipurpose (recommended) Allows you to use this list for purposes other than mail.
   - Access Control List Only Only used in Access Control Lists. Not relevant to the Personal Address Book.
   - Mail Only Used to define mailing lists. This is the selection you choose for groups.
   - Deny List Only Only used by Notes administrator. Not applicable to the Personal Address Book.

6. Type a short description of the group in the Description field. Although this is not a mandatory field, it might be helpful later when you try to remember why you created this group in the first place.
7. Type the names of the members in the Members field, separating the names with commas. Or click the down arrow next to the field and select the names from your Personal Address Book.
8. Click the Save button and then click Close. Or click Close and then click Yes when you want to save document.
9. Close the address book by pressing your Esc key.

After you create the group, you can use it when you address memos. Simply type the name of the group in the To field (Typeahead will complete the name as you type), and Notes will send your e-mail to all the people in the group. If a person drops out of the group, or a new person is added, you can edit the group document by double-clicking on the group in your address book and selecting Edit from the menu. By using the group name when addressing your mail, you can save a lot of typing.

Too Much Mail? Lotus Notes saves a copy of your mail by default. Including yourself in a group would result in your having *two* copies of a mail message, the one you *saved* and the one you *received* as a member of the group.

Addressing Mail to the Internet

The Internet is an international network of networks. People all over the world use the Internet to gather information and to communicate. If you use the Internet to send mail, you have to have an Internet address with the Internet service provider through which you connect to the Internet. Many Internet users in the United States belong to services such as CompuServe, Prodigy, or America Online. For example, a typical America Online address is SueAnnB@aol.com.

When you create a Person document for an Internet addressee, you'll select Internet mail as the mail type.

If you can access Internet mail at work, you should check with your Lotus Notes administrator for assistance with Internet addressing. A typical Internet address would read name@domain.com where name is the name of the person you're sending to, domain is the name of their domain and .com is the type of domain, in this case a commercial entity. Other domain types include .edu for educational institutions, .org for nonprofit organizations and .gov for government organizations.

In this lesson, you learned about the two address books, how to create Person Documents, and how to address mail to people outside of your network or on another server. In the next lesson, you'll learn more about sending mail messages.

LESSON 9

Sending Mail Messages

In this lesson, you learn how to apply mail delivery options. You also learn how to set Send options.

Using Delivery Options

You can set several delivery options before you send your mail. Those delivery options can:

- Let recipients know your message is important.
- Place a digital signature on your message.
- Encrypt your message.
- Set delivery priorities.
- Request confirmation that the message was received.
- Request confirmation that the message was read.
- Prevent addressees from copying the message.

Encrypt Sounds like you need to put on your magic decoder ring! When you choose to encrypt a message, Lotus Notes scrambles the message and only the recipient has the key to unscramble it. Since your message travels from your PC to the Lotus Notes server, and then to the PC of the recipient, encrypting the message will prevent anyone who may be working at the Lotus Notes server from reading your message.

To set delivery options, click the Delivery Options button on the action bar. The Delivery Options dialog box appears (see Figure 9.1).

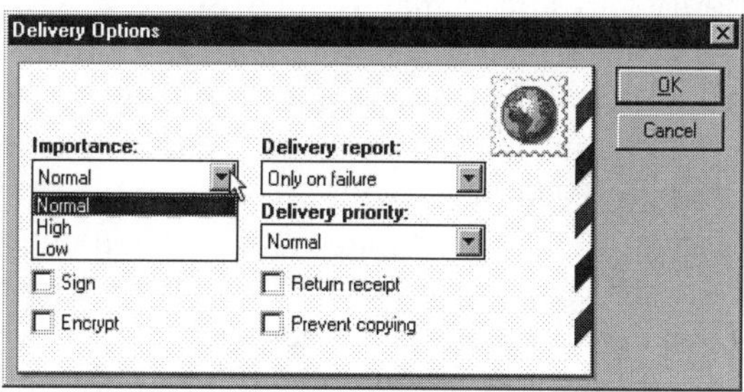

FIGURE 9.1 The Delivery Options dialog box.

Setting Importance lets the recipient know how important your message is. Choose Normal, High, or Low in the Importance drop-down list. If you choose High, the recipient will see a red exclamation mark ! next to your mail message in their Inbox (see Figure 9.2). Choosing Normal or Low does not affect how your mail message appears in the recipients Inbox at all.

To add a digital signature, which lets the recipient know you are the person who created the message, choose Sign in the Delivery Options dialog box.

To encrypt your mail, select Encrypt in the Delivery Options dialog box. In order to encrypt the mail, the person you are mailing to must exist in the Public Address Book, as encryption is accomplished by using a number called the Public Key that is stored in each Person document in the Public Address Book.

! Dorothy Burke 07/15/96 testing

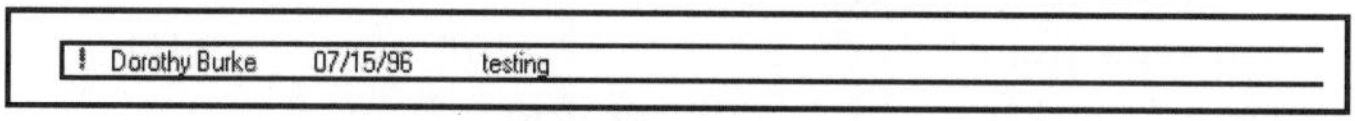

FIGURE 9.2 The High importance indicator.

The Delivery priority determines how the Lotus Notes server will handle your mail when it receives your message on the way to the recipient.

Delivery priority only affects mail that crosses servers, such as mail that is sent to a recipient via the Internet or other Lotus Notes servers. It can override the regularly scheduled time that servers call to exchange mail. If your mail is urgent, setting the Delivery priority to High forces your server to immediately call another server and deliver your mail. This is very useful if you have an urgent message. If you set the Delivery priority to Normal (the default value), your mail travels across servers at the predetermined time(s) set by your Lotus Notes administrator. If you set the Delivery priority to Low, your mail will be sent between the hours of 2 a.m. and 6 a.m., the default time for low priority, unless your Notes administrator has changed that time. This is a good option if you're sending large attachments (as discussed in Lesson 13). Using a Low priority sends this mail during off peak hours.

The Delivery report (see Figure 9.3) provides different information about the delivery of your message to the recipient:

Only on failure (the default value) Returns a delivery failure report to you if your mail can't be delivered.

Confirm delivery Returns a confirmation notice indicating that your mail delivery was successful. If you asked for a confirm delivery report for each mail message you sent, you'll have an Inbox full of notices! Use this choice sparingly.

Trace entire path Returns a report telling you the path your mail took to get to its recipient. If you are having problems with your mail, your Lotus Notes administrator might ask you to use this option to determine the source of the problem.

None Mutes the delivery report. You'll get no delivery reports at all—even if your mail could not be delivered to the recipient.

FIGURE 9.3 A Delivery failure report.

Simply because a person has *received* your mail doesn't mean that she has *read* it. Selecting Return receipt in the Delivery Options dialog box notifies you that the recipient has read your message. This works only for other Lotus Notes Mail users, not across the Internet.

The Prevent copying option in the Delivery Options dialog box restricts what happens to your message once it is received by other Notes users. You can prevent the recipient from copying the message to the Windows Clipboard, forwarding the message to another person, creating a reply with history (as described in Lesson 11), or printing your message. Again, this only applies to other Notes Mail users.

Once you have chosen your delivery options, click OK to apply them to your message.

CREATING MOOD STAMPS

Pay special attention to the Mood Stamps option on the Delivery Options dialog box. You can use Mood Stamps to tell your recipients what type of mood your message holds. When they view their Inbox, they'll see icons to the left of your mail message indicating your mail message "mood" (see Figure 9.4). Notes creates these icons for all moods except Normal.

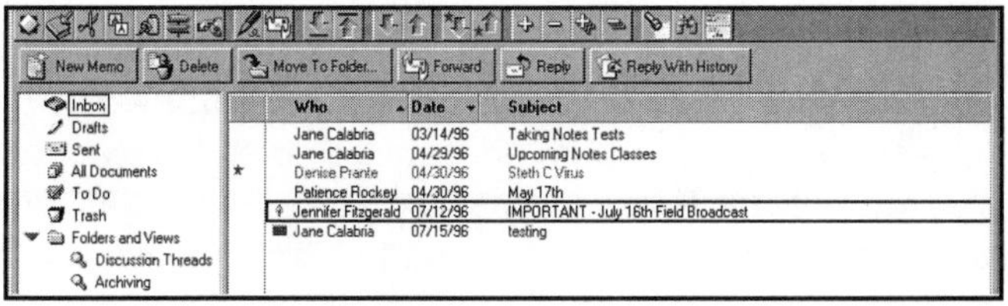

FIGURE 9.4 Mood Stamp displays in the Inbox.

To attach a mood stamp to your mail message, click the Delivery Options button on the Action bar. In the Delivery Options dialog box, select a message type from the Mood Stamp drop-down list: Normal, Personal, Confidential, Private, Thank You, Flame, Good Job!, Joke, FYI, Question, or Reminder. Then click OK.

SETTING SEND OPTIONS

You can find less frequently used mail options by choosing Actions, Special Options from the menu. From the Special Options dialog box, you can set options to automatically delete mail messages from your Mail database, archive messages, and request a reply by date (see Figure 9.5).

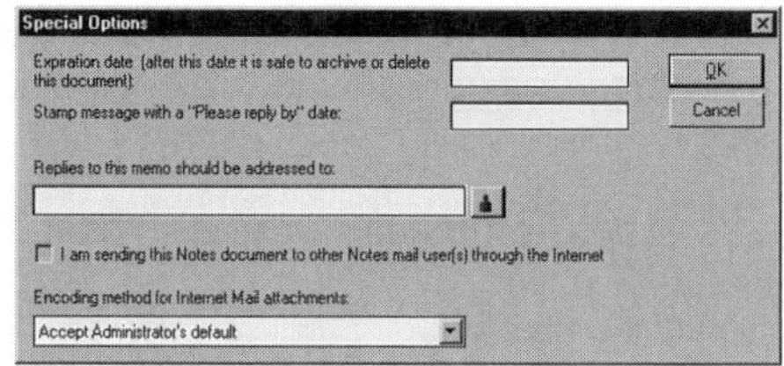

FIGURE 9.5 The Special Options dialog box.

If you want to automatically delete or archive your memo, type a date in the Expiration date field of the Special Options dialog box. Archiving is discussed in Lesson 12.

To request a response to your mail message by a certain date, you can enter a date in the Stamp message with a "Please reply by" date box. That request will be sent as part of the mail message.

If you'd like the response to your mail to be sent to someone else (not you), you can indicate that information by filling out the Replies to this memo should be addressed to box. For example, if you type **Mary Jane Kane** in this box, you see a note at the top of your memo that says Please respond to Mary Jane Kane.

Your Lotus Notes mail message appears as plain text when received by someone on the Internet. That's just the way it works;

formatting options don't always interpret well. But if you send mail to another Lotus Notes Mail user through the Internet, he can see your text formatting if you select the I am sending this Notes document to other Notes Mail user(s) through the Internet option. Making this selection doesn't guarantee the transfer of formatting options, since your message may travel through many different servers. But failing to select this option guarantees that the Lotus Notes Mail formatting options will be lost—regardless of the product used by the recipient.

To close the Special Options dialog box, click OK.

SAVING COPIES

To send and *file* your mail at the same time, click on the Send and File button on the Action bar. With this option, Notes will file your sent copy in the folder you specify, as opposed to your Sent folder. When you choose Send and File, the Move to Folder dialog box appears which lists your available folders. Select the folder you wish to use.

To remove a document from a folder without deleting it from the database, choose Actions, Remove from Folder.

Some companies restrict the sizes of mail databases. If your company is concerned with space, you might want to disable the "Always keep a copy" option of user preferences and have Notes prompt you with an option to save a copy every time you send a new message.

In this lesson, you learned how to use delivery options and how to set send options for mail. You also learned how to file a copy of your mail message at the time you send it. In the next lesson, you learn about reading mail you receive.

Lesson 10 Reading and Printing Mail

In this lesson, you learn how to use the Preview pane and change views while you are reading your mail. You'll also learn about read marks and printing.

Opening Your Mail

No Mail? If you're new to Lotus Notes Mail, you may not have mail in your Inbox. In preparation for this lesson, call your co-workers and ask them to send you mail so you have mail in your Inbox to work with during this lesson (or send some mail to yourself).

There are a couple of ways to access your incoming mail.

- From the workspace, you can double-click your Mail database icon. When the database opens (by default, at your Inbox view), you can double-click on the piece of mail you want to read.
- Click the Inbox icon located on the bottom right of the status bar. Select Scan Unread Mail. This will open the first unread mail message in your Inbox.

When you finish reading your mail message, you can press the Esc key to return to your Inbox, or you can continue to read unopened (unread) messages by using the SmartIcons. Once you open a mail message, there are four SmartIcons to assist you in navigating through your mail, without the need to return to the Inbox.

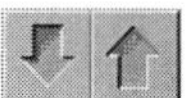

Use the *plain* up and down arrow icons to navigate to the next or the previous mail message.

The up and down arrow icons with stars take you to the next or the previous *unread* message.

When you finish reading your mail, you'll be returned to your Inbox.

UNDERSTANDING READ MARKS

When you see your messages listed in the Inbox, you can tell at a glance which messages you've read. Mail messages you haven't read appear in red and have a star located to the left of the mail message. Once you open and read the message, the star disappears and the mail message appears in black in your Inbox. Figure 10.1 shows mail messages in the Inbox that have been read and some that haven't.

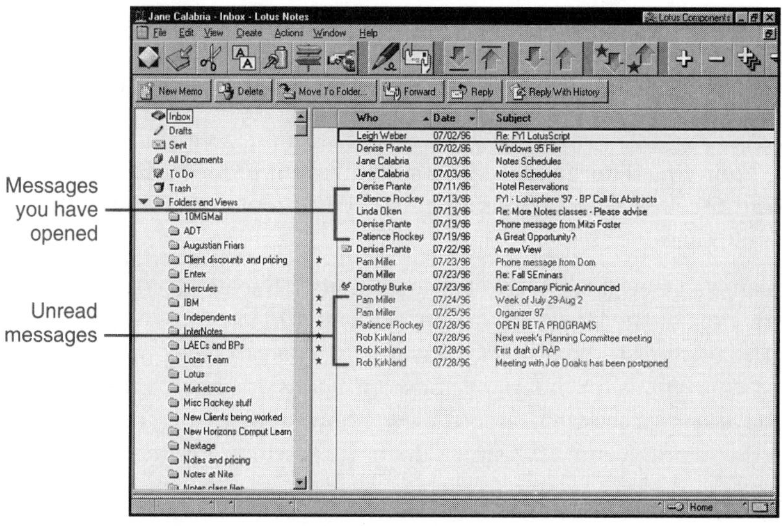

FIGURE 10.1 Read Marks display in Inbox.

CHANGING VIEWS

As you learned in Lesson 3, there are several ways to view your mail. You can sort how mail appears in your Inbox by using the sorting icons located on the column headers of the Who and the Date columns. The default sort for the Inbox is by date, with the most current date at the bottom of your screen. So, new mail appears at the bottom of the list. If you click the triangle located in the header of the Date column, the triangle turns to a blue color, and your mail sorts with the most current mail first, or at the top of the list.

If you click the triangle located in the Who column, the triangle turns blue and your mail sorts alphabetically by the first name of the person who sent it. This view is useful when you need to find a mail message sent to you from a particular person, and perhaps you don't remember the date or the subject.

You can elect to have only unread mail show in your Inbox. To do so, select View, Show, and Unread Only from the menu. Now only those mail messages you have not read will appear in your Inbox. You can turn on and off the option to show only unread mail at any time. You can also see all of the mail by selecting the All Documents view.

Once you've read messages, you'll probably want to reply, delete, or file those messages. Lessons 11 and 12 cover replying to and filing messages.

You can also view a list of *selected* documents. To select documents, click to the left of the document listing in your Inbox. A check mark appears next to that document. You can select one, many, contiguous (in order), or non-contiguous documents. Once you have several selected, choose View, Show, and Selected only from the menu. Figure 10.2 shows documents selected in the Inbox.

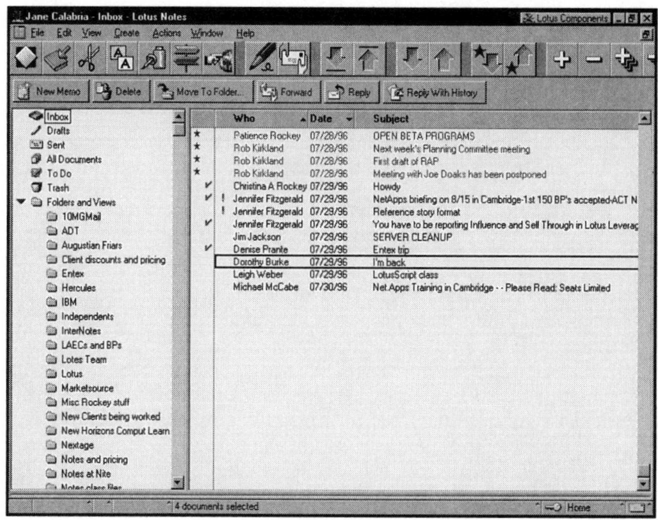

FIGURE 10.2 Selecting documents in the Inbox.

USING THE PREVIEW PANE

You may prefer to read your mail by using the *Preview pane* so you can view a mail message while you still see the Navigator pane and the list of documents in your Inbox. The Preview pane splits your Inbox into three panels. To turn on the Preview pane, select View and Document Preview from the menu. The Document Preview pane activates (see Figure 10.3).

The Document Preview pane is adjustable. You may decide you want to see more of the message and less of the Inbox documents list. To size the Preview pane, place your cursor on the gray horizontal line that stretches across the screen above the mail message; when your cursor changes to a sizing cursor (a double-headed arrow), click and drag the line up or down, depending on whether you want this section to be larger or smaller.

You can use the scrollbars located in any three of these panels (the Navigator pane, the Documents pane, or the Preview pane) to scroll through the contents of each window. What displays

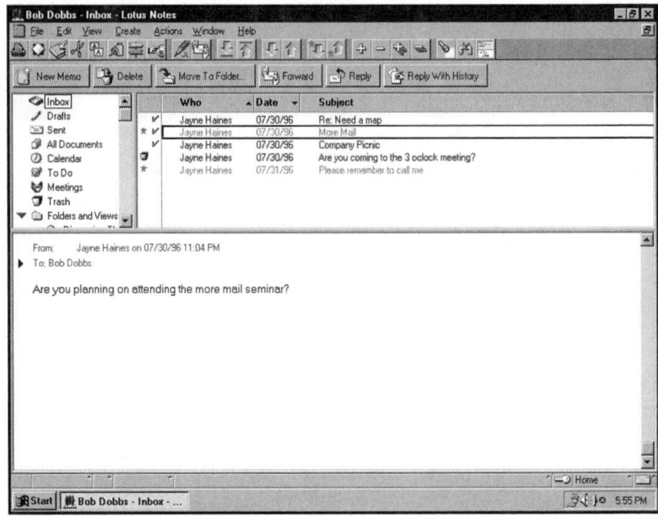

FIGURE 10.3 The Preview pane.

in the Preview pane is driven by which mail message you have selected in the Documents pane. To preview mail in your Inbox you can move through the documents located in your Inbox by:

- Using your up or down arrow keys on your keyboard.
- Using the Tab key (or Shift+Tab to move backward).
- Using the Navigator SmartIcons located on the toolbar.
- Using your mouse to select a mail message.

Previewing Is Not Reading Using the Preview pane to read your mail does not really count as reading mail. Lotus Notes will not mark the mail as "read" if you've only previewed it. Many people find previewing a quick way to read their mail.

You can configure the Preview pane to look differently than the three panel split you see here. Select View, Arrange Preview to see the Preview Pane dialog box for your options. (See Figure 10.4.)

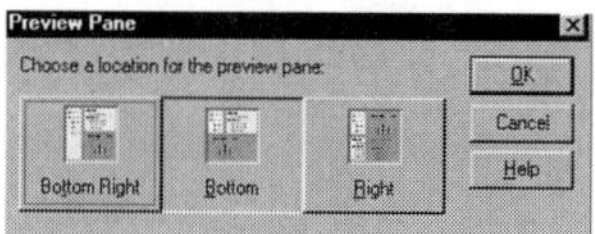

FIGURE 10.4 The Preview Pane dialog box.

The default selection is Bottom, which refers to the position of the Preview pane. You can select Bottom Right or Right, and you can also resize these panels after you make your selection.

PRINTING MAIL

You can print one or several pieces of mail at a time. Like many Windows products, you can activate the Print command in several ways. In Lesson 3, you added the Print SmartIcon to your toolbar; using the Print icon is one way to print a single copy of mail. To print more than one mail message at a time, select those messages by clicking next to each one in the left column of the Inbox view. This will place a check mark next to the mail message. Then print by using one of the following methods:

- Click once on the Print SmartIcon. This will print one copy of the mail message you have open.
- Hold down the Ctrl key while pressing the letter p. This also prints one copy of the mail message you have open.
- Select File, Print from the menu. This gives you the option to print multiple copies, headers and footer, change the orientation of the printer, or change the printer selection.

If you want to print more than one copy of your mail, choose File, Print from the menu. In the File Print dialog box (see Figure 10.5), indicate the number of copies you want to print in Copies box. Then click OK to print the copies.

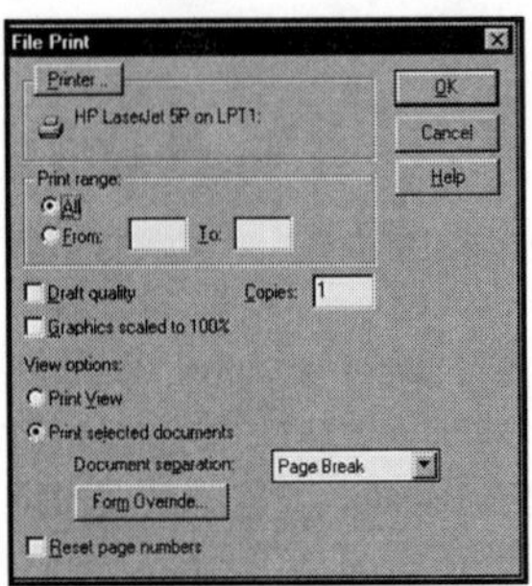

FIGURE 10.5 The File Print dialog box.

It may be useful, at times, to print a view. To print a view, select File, Print from the menu. In the View options portion of the Print dialog box, click Print View. Click OK to print.

In this lesson, you learned how to work with Read Marks and set your preferences for scanning unread documents. You also learned about various views and previewing mail. You also learned how to print your mail. In the next lesson, you learn how to reply to mail.

REPLYING TO MAIL

LESSON 11

In this lesson, you learn about options for replying to mail. You also learn how to add people to your address book.

UNDERSTANDING REPLIES

Often, your mail messages require a response from you. Responding to mail is similar to creating a new mail message, that is, the form that you use is the same as the form you use when you create a new message. But when you reply to mail, you have several options, including the option to include the text from the mail message to which you are replying. When you do reply to a mail message, try to keep in mind the e-mail etiquette covered in Lesson 2. If the message to which you reply was originally sent to more than one person, you might consider sending your reply to all of the people on the original distribution.

USING REPLY OPTIONS

You can find two buttons for replying to mail on the Action bar of your Inbox: Reply and Reply With History. To see these buttons, double-click the Mail database icon in your workspace; the mail Inbox opens. Double-click the mail message that you want to reply to. The mail message appears, similar to the one shown in Figure 11.1.

There is a third option, Reply To All, that allows you to reply to all the recipients of the original mail message. You'll learn how to use all three reply options in the following sections.

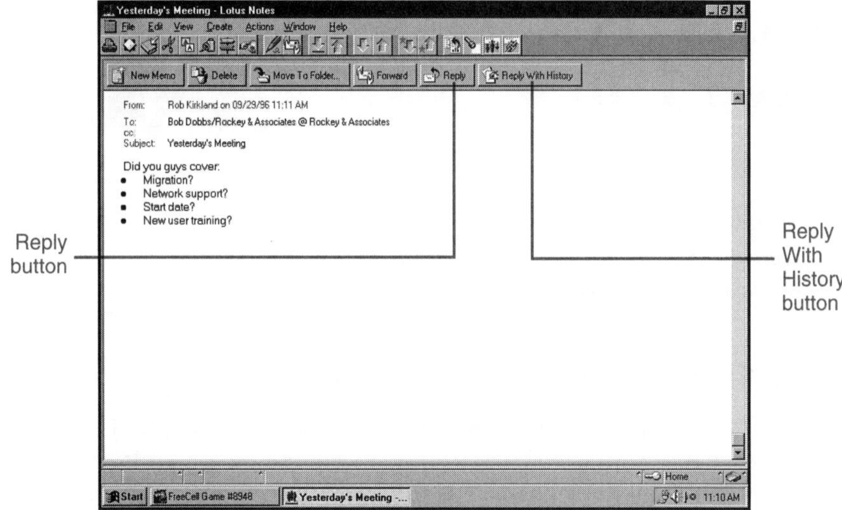

FIGURE 11.1 An opened mail message requiring a reply.

REPLY

To respond to a message using the Reply option:

1. Click the Reply button located on the Action bar. A new mail message appears ready for you to fill in your reply (see Figure 11.2). The To field and the Subject line are already filled in with the recipients' names and the subject of the previous message.
2. Fill in the body of the mail message; then click the Send button located on the Action bar to send the message.

Since this particular message was one in which the sender asked a lot of questions, it might be helpful to see the original message on your screen while typing your reply. To view the original message while typing a response:

1. Open a message to which you want to reply by double-clicking it in your Inbox.
2. Position your cursor on the gray bar located at the top of the status bar (near the bottom of your screen).

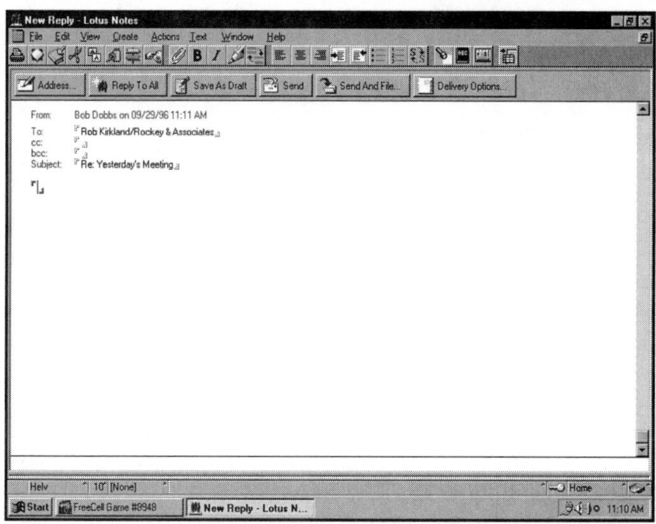

FIGURE 11.2 Replying to a mail message.

3. When you see the double-arrow sizing pointer, click-and-drag the gray bar up the screen.
4. At about halfway up the screen, release the mouse button.
5. You can now see the original message on the bottom of your screen (see Figure 11.3) and your reply form on the top of the screen.

In Figure 11.3, you can see the results of splitting your screen this way. It's now easier to remember what you want to say when you're replying to this piece of mail.

REPLY WITH HISTORY

There is another way to reply to this particular piece of mail. You can save a lot of typing by answering questions with one word such as "yes" or "no." But if you respond in that way, the person receiving your response may not understand which questions you're responding to.

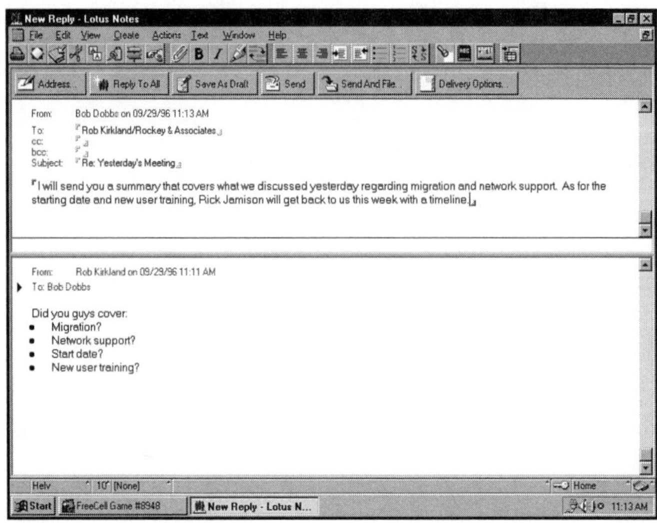

FIGURE 11.3 Viewing the original mail message while replying.

To keep your typing to a minimum and to help the original sender remember what this message was all about, you can select Reply With History on the Action bar or send your response back with the original message that was sent to you. Figure 11.4 shows the result of this option. You can complete the reply form, and the original memo will be sent along with your reply.

After you complete the Reply With History, click the Send button located on the Action bar to send this message.

REPLY TO ALL

The third reply option, Reply To All, does not appear on the Action bar where you find Reply and Reply With History. In the example for this reply, Rob had sent a mail message to me and included Dorothy in the cc: field. Obviously, Rob wanted Dorothy to know that he was asking me for information. When I chose the Reply and the Reply With History options, only Rob's name (the sender) was filled in on my mail memo. If I chose Reply To All as my reply option, then Dorothy would have been included in the reply. Her name would again appear in the field in which the sender had originally included it, in this case, in the cc: field.

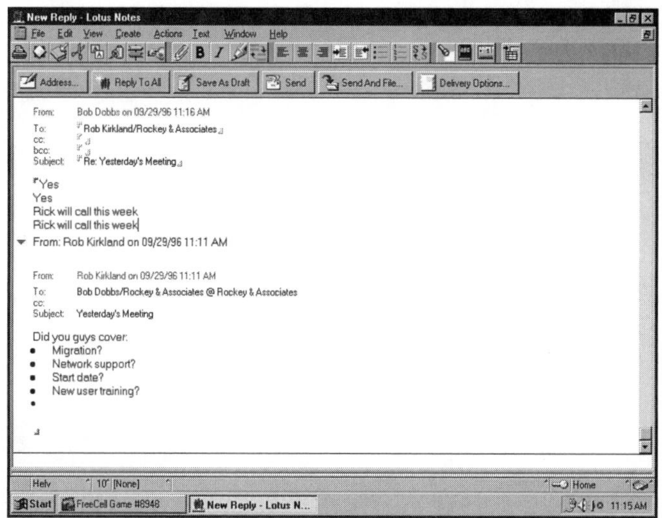

FIGURE 11.4 Using the Reply With History option.

The Reply To All option appears on the action bar *after* you select Reply or Reply To All. When the new mail message appears ready for a reply, the Action bar includes a Reply To All button. Click the Reply To All button, and all original recipients of this message will be automatically filled in. Figure 11.5 shows the results of choosing the Reply To All option once the New Reply form is on-screen.

Forget to Reply To All? It's easy to forget to use the Reply To All option since it does not appear on the first Action bar while reading mail. If you send your reply without using Reply To All, you can re-create your reply using Reply To All, or you can *forward* your saved copy to the others who were in the original distribution list. You learn about forwarding later in this lesson.

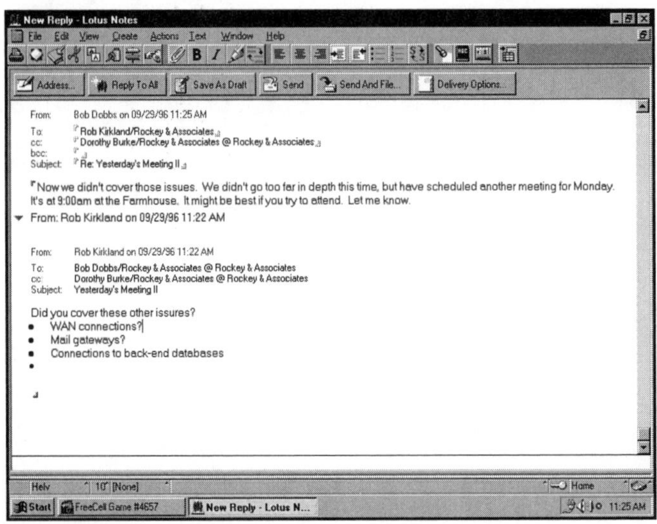

FIGURE 11.5 Selecting the Reply To All option fills in the recipients of the original mail message.

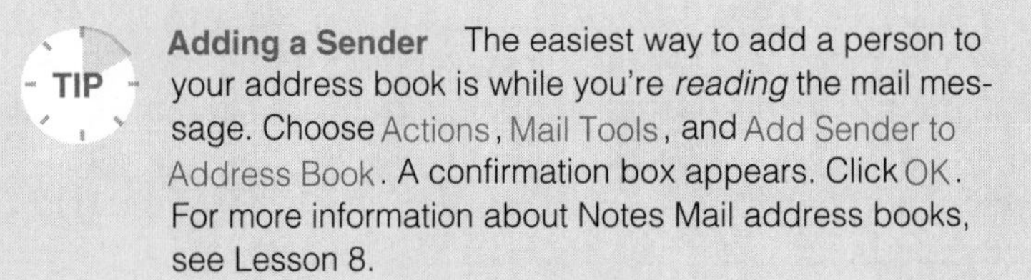

Adding a Sender The easiest way to add a person to your address book is while you're *reading* the mail message. Choose Actions, Mail Tools, and Add Sender to Address Book. A confirmation box appears. Click OK. For more information about Notes Mail address books, see Lesson 8.

FORWARDING MAIL

You may receive a mail message that you want to *forward* to someone else. To forward a mail message, open the message and click the Forward button on the Action bar. Fill in the address portion of the message, and include any message you want to send along with the original. Send the mail as you would any other piece of mail.

In this lesson, you learned the options for replying to mail. In the next lesson, you learn how to delete mail and use folders.

Managing Mail Messages

In this lesson, you learn about deleting mail messages, creating folders, using the Discussion Thread view, archiving old mail, and viewing sent mail.

Deleting Mail

To keep your Mail database manageable, you should make it a practice to clear out old messages periodically. If you're not sure if you'll need the message again, archive it. If you know you won't need the message any longer, delete it.

In Lotus Notes, deleting messages is a two-step process. First you mark the message for deletion; then you remove it by emptying the Trash.

You can mark messages for deletion while you're reading them, or you can do it from the View pane. To delete a message while you are in read mode:

1. In the opened message, click the Delete button on the action bar, or press the Delete key on your keyboard.
2. Lotus Notes marks that message for deletion, and your next message appears.

You Didn't Mean to Click the Delete Button So far, you've only *marked* the message for deletion. If you didn't mean to mark it for deletion, open the Trash folder, select the message, and press the Delete key to remove the mark.

3. Continue reading the rest of your messages, deleting those you don't want to keep.

To mark messages for deletion while you are in the View pane (or Inbox), you must first highlight the message, or if you are deleting multiple documents, select the messages using one of the following methods:

- Select a message you want to delete by clicking the document in the view. Then press the Delete key or use the Delete button.
- If you want to select several messages in a row, click the first message and drag up or down the left side of the messages. This will place a check mark next to all of the messages you drag past. You can also select messages that are not below each other, by placing a check mark next to them.
- Choose Edit, Select All to select all of the messages in the view.

If you accidentally selected a document you didn't mean to mark, click the check mark to remove it. To remove all the check marks, choose Edit, Deselect All.

To mark the selected documents for deletion, press the Delete key or click the Delete button on the Action bar. A trash can appears next to each item you have marked for deletion (see Figure 12.1). When you exit the database, you may be prompted with a message asking if you want to permanently delete these messages. Click Yes.

CREATING FOLDERS

When you frequently use your e-mail at work, you'll receive many messages. You might not want to delete every mail message, but you can organize your work by creating folders to store your mail messages. You can create whatever folders you need and then put the appropriate messages into the folders, much like organizing a file cabinet.

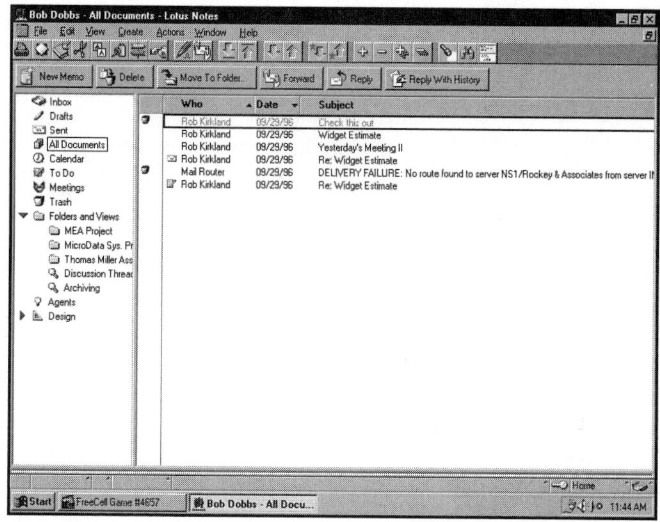

FIGURE 12.1 Messages marked for deletion.

To create a folder:

1. Choose Create, Folder from the menu bar.
2. In the Create Folder dialog box, enter a name in the Folder name box (see Figure 12.2).

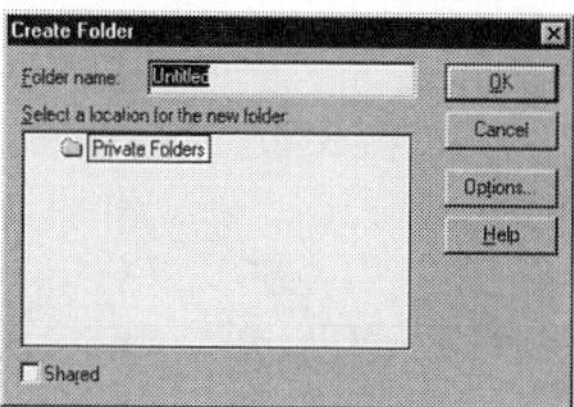

FIGURE 12.2 The Create Folder dialog box.

3. If you want to put the new folder inside an existing one (like putting a manila folder inside a Pendaflex® folder in a filing cabinet), click that folder from the Select a location for the new folder list box.

Don't Check Shared Unless you are an Applications Developer (one who designs Notes databases), you don't have the rights to create "*shared*" folders. Shared folders are accessible to many people. Folders you'll make are *private* folders—for your use only.

4. Click OK.

To place mail messages in the folder, you can:

- Drag them
- Use the menu commands
- Use the action bar

To drag documents to folders from your Inbox:

1. Select the document (or documents) you want to move into the folder.
2. Click the document and drag it until it is over the folder.
3. When the mouse pointer is over the folder, it changes to a small document icon with a plus (+) sign over it. Then release the mouse button.

Dragging a mail message moves the message to a folder, removing it from the current folder (in this case, your Inbox). If you hold down the Control key while dragging, you can add the message to a different folder, leaving a copy of it in its current folder.

Documents or Views? In Lesson 1 you learned that everything in a Lotus Notes database is stored in a document. Mail messages are no exception. Technically, we call them documents. In e-mail terms, we call them messages.

Other ways to move mail messages are to use the menu commands. To move a mail message to another folder using the menu:

1. If you're in the Inbox, select the documents you want to put in a folder (if you're reading the message, only that document will move to the folder).
2. Choose Actions, Move to Folder or click the Move to Folder button on the Action bar.
3. In the Move To Folder dialog box (see Figure 12.3), click a folder name in the Select a folder list box (click the Create New Folder button if you haven't made the folder yet).

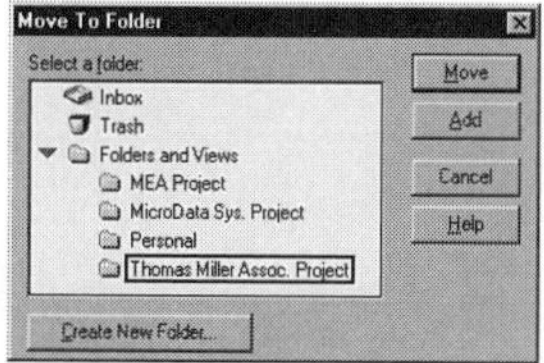

FIGURE 12.3 The Move To Folder dialog box.

4. Click the Add button to put the mail message into the folder without removing it from other folders. Or click the Move button to put the mail message into the folder while removing it from other folders (you cannot remove the message from a view).

USING THE DISCUSSION THREAD VIEW

With mail messages, you frequently develop *conversations*. Joe sends a message to Mary, Tim, and Jack inquiring about their vacation plans. Mary replies that she is going to Cape Cod for a week in August. Joe replies to Mary that he knows a great place for dinner on the Cape. Meanwhile, Tim responds to Joe's original message, as does Jack. A conversation is born.

Messages that are responses to previous memos will have a Re: at the beginning of the subject and a Document Link icon. The icon links you back to the message being replied to.

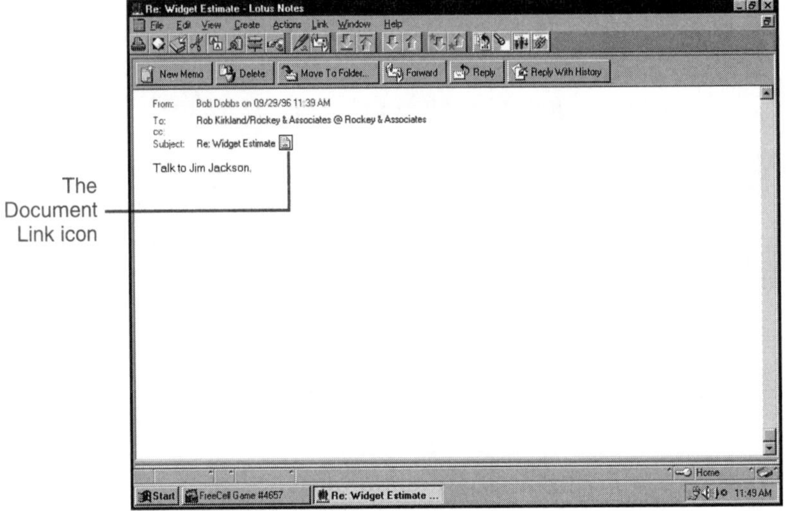

FIGURE 12.4 Message that is a reply.

If you have a long conversation, the best way to follow it from beginning to end is to look in the Discussion Thread view. Click the Discussion Thread View icon in the Navigator pane to see the list of documents organized by conversations (see Figure 12.5). The subject line of reply messages appears indented, and replies to replies appear further indented.

ARCHIVING MAIL

There are several strategies for reducing the size of your Mail database, and *archiving* old mail messages is one of them. Archiving stores the old messages in another database, making your Mail database more manageable. You can have these messages archived automatically or do it manually.

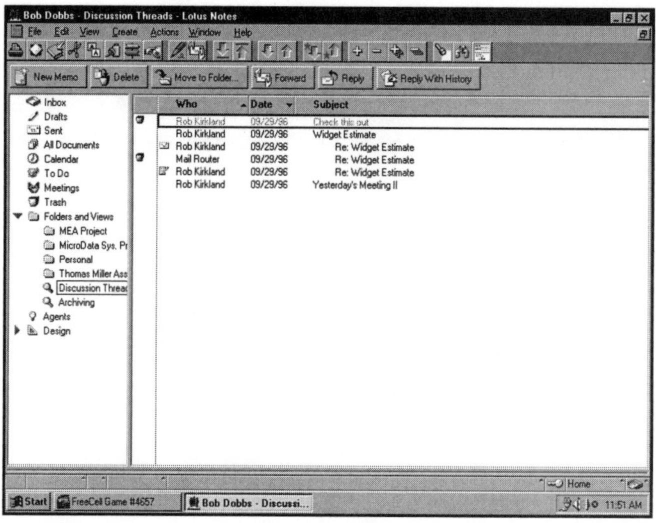

FIGURE 12.5 The Discussion Thread view.

To set up automatic archiving:

1. In the Navigator pane, double-click the Archiving view icon to open that view.
2. Click the Setup Archive button on the Action bar (see Figure 12.6).
3. The Archive Profile form appears, as shown in Figure 12.7. Complete the Archive Profile form. You can fill in any of the following options:

    Check Archive Expired documents and set how many days before a document is archived.

    Check Archive documents which have no activity and set a time limit (in days).

    Check whether you want to Generate an Archive Log each time an archive occurs.

    Check Include document links if you want to add them to the archive.

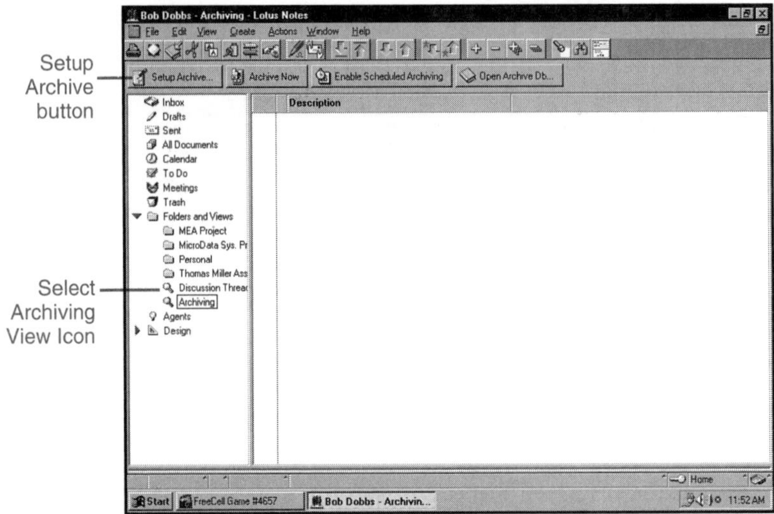

FIGURE 12.6 The Setup Archive button.

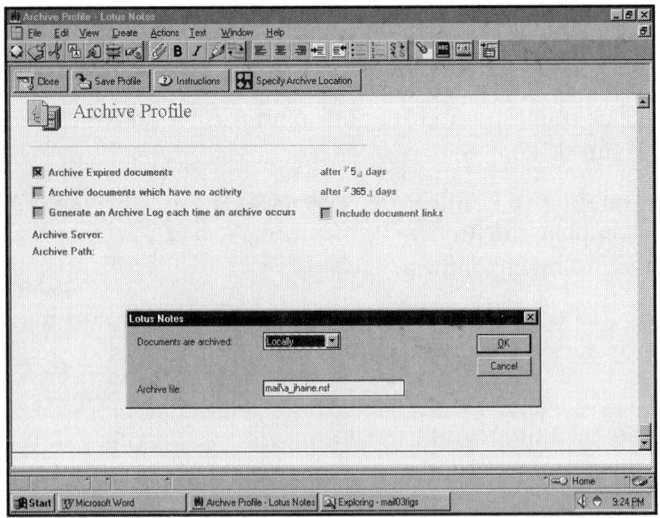

FIGURE 12.7 The Archive Profile form.

Choose whether the documents will be archived Locally or On Server by clicking the appropriate radio button (the small round button in front of the option; you can only choose one). You must be allowed to create databases on the server to create the Archive database there. You may not have this ability.

You may enter the name of the database file, if you don't want to use the one Lotus Notes generates automatically.

4. Click the Save Profile button on the Action bar.
5. When the dialog box appears saying that the Archive database has been created, click OK.
6. Click the Close button on the Action bar.
7. Switch temporarily to another folder or view in your Mail database and then back to the Archiving view.
8. Click the Enable Scheduling Archiving button on the Action bar to activate the automatic archiving.

If you decide to turn off the automatic archiving, open the Archiving view and click the Disable Scheduled Archiving button on the Action bar.

You don't have to wait for Lotus Notes to archive your messages based on the schedule you set up. Select the messages that you want to archive and choose Actions, Mail Tools, Archive Selected Documents.

Once you have documents in the Archive database, you may view them by opening the database. From the Archiving view, click the Open Archive Db button on the Action bar. Then simply open the messages you want to read.

If you set up an Archive Log in your Archive Profile document and chose to include document links, you can also view the archived messages by opening the log. From the Archiving view, open the Archive Log that has the message you want to see. Click the Link icon, read the message, and then close it.

VIEWING SENT MAIL

If you save your mail when you send it, Lotus Notes automatically stores it in the Sent folder. To view all the messages there, click the Sent Folder icon.

In this lesson, you learned about managing your mail messages by deleting or archiving old messages, viewing conversations in the Discussion Thread view, seeing the messages you sent in the Sent folder, and creating your own folders. In the next lesson, you learn about attaching non-Notes files to your messages.

LESSON 13

Attaching Files

In this lesson, you learn how to create and manage file attachments. You'll also learn how to detach and launch file attachments.

Understanding Attachments

There may be times when you want to send a file to someone through e-mail. That file might be a Lotus Notes database, a spreadsheet, a word processing document, a compressed file, a graphic file, or a scanned photograph of your grandchildren—just about any type of file. In Lotus Notes, you can attach an entire file within the rich text field, or body, of your mail message and send it. The file you attach is a *copy*, so your original stays intact on your computer.

The user who receives your mail can *detach* your file and save it. If the recipient has the same application program in which the file was created, she can *launch* the application. Launching opens the file in its *native* application.

Attachments can only be placed in rich text fields and the body of the mail message is the only rich text field in the Mail Message form.

Creating Attachments

To attach a file to a Lotus Notes mail message:

1. Create the mail message. Make sure your insertion point (cursor) is in the message body at the exact point where you want the attachment to appear.

2. Choose File, Attach, or click the File Attach SmartIcon. The Create Attachments dialog box appears as shown in Figure 13.1.

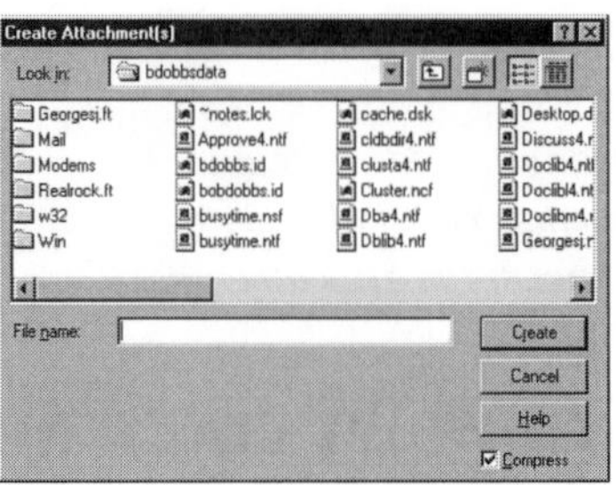

FIGURE 13.1 The Create Attachments dialog box.

3. In the Create Attachments dialog box, enter the name of the file you want to attach in the File name box and then specify its location by choosing the correct drive and directory, or folder. Or specify the location first and then select the file name from the list.

4. The compress file box is enabled by default. You should leave this box checked.

Compressed files will transfer faster than those that are not compressed. However, it might take a little longer to attach the file to your message because Notes compresses the file during the attachment process. A compressed file will also take up less disk space on the server.

5. Click the Create button. The attached file appears as an icon within the body of your mail message.

Click and Drag Attachments In Windows 3.1, you can attach a file using the File Manager; in Windows 95, you use the Windows Explorer. Simply set up your desktop so you can see two windows at once (choose Windows, Tile in Windows 3.1; click the right mouse button on the taskbar in Windows 95 and select Tile Vertically or Tile Horizontally). Create the mail message in the Lotus Notes window. Then drag the File icon from the File Manager or Windows Explorer window into your Lotus Notes window and drop it into your document.

The appearance of the icon depends on the type of file it represents and whether or not you have the original software that this file was created in installed on your PC. If you are attaching a Lotus 1-2-3 file, you'll see a Lotus 1-2-3 icon in your mail message. If the file is a Microsoft Word file, you see a Microsoft Word icon in your mail message. If you don't have native software installed for that file, you see a generic document icon.

When you receive mail that has an attachment, a Paper Clip icon appears next to the mail message in your Inbox. (See Figure 13.2.)

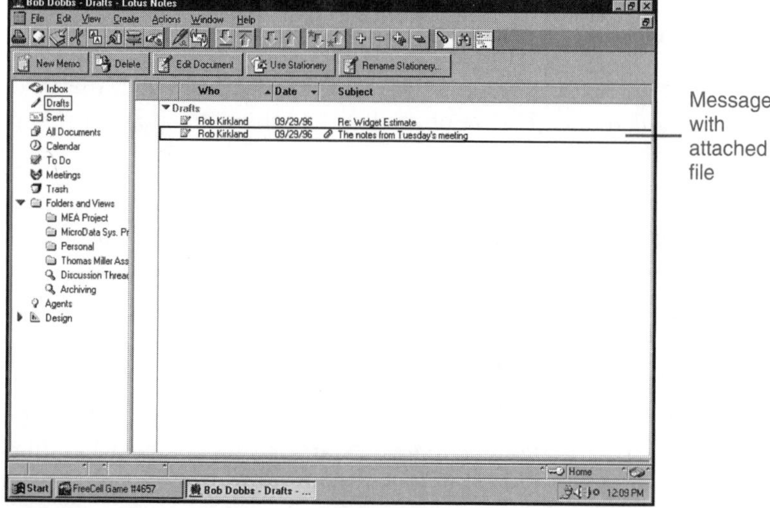

FIGURE 13.2 A Paper Clip icon in the Inbox shows a mail message with an attachment.

VIEWING, DETACHING, OR LAUNCHING AN ATTACHMENT

When you receive an attached file, you can view the file to see what it is, even if you don't have the application that runs it. Open the mail message, double-click the attachment icon, and click the View button in the Properties box (see Figure 13.3). Be aware that when you view the file this way, the files you see are unformatted; they're straight text only. Once you finish looking

Esc

You Can't View the Lotus WordPro Document Attachment? WordPro is one exception; you must have WordPro installed in order to view a WordPro document.

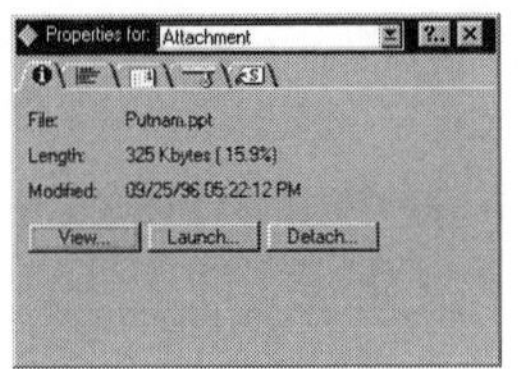

FIGURE 13.3 The Attachment Properties box.

The Properties box also gives you information about the attached file: its name, the size of the file, and the date and time it was last modified.

If you want to look at an attached file in the application in which it was created, you can launch the application from within mail, or detach it.

1. Double-click the File icon.
2. Click the Detach button on the Properties box.
3. In the Save Attachment dialog box (see Figure 13.4), specify the file name you want to give the detached file, and the drive and directory (or folder) where you want to store it.

4. Click the Detach button in the Save Attachment dialog box; close the Properties box.

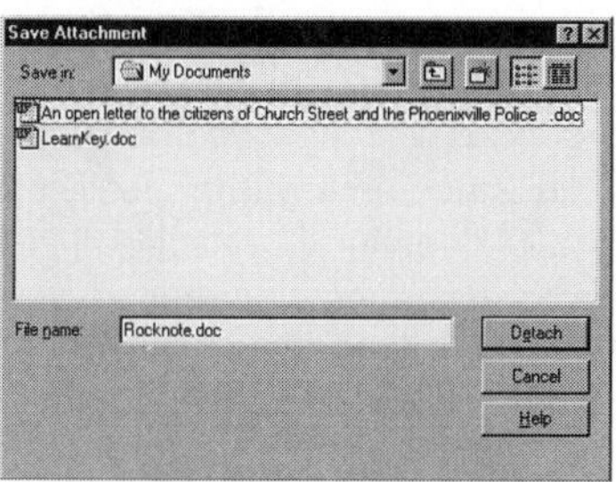

FIGURE 13.4 The Save Attachment dialog box.

To detach more than one file, select the file icons of the files you want to detach (hold down the Shift key and click each icon). Then choose Attachment, Detach All Selected. Or to detach all the attached files, choose Attachment, Detach All. The Save Attachments dialog box appears as shown in Figure 13.5. Specify the drive and directory, or folder, where you want to save the files. Click OK.

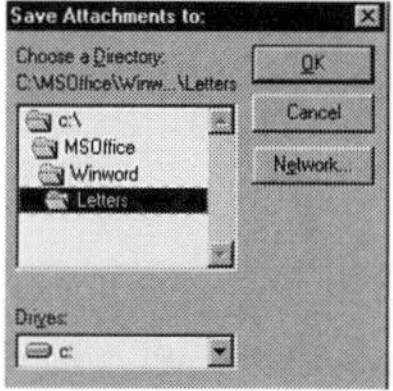

FIGURE 13.5 The Save Attachments to dialog box.

To launch an attachment, double-click the attachment icon and then click the Launch button on the Properties box. You can then view the document and/or make changes. You can save it or print it from the application. You can close the application when you finish with the file. Lotus Notes and your mail message remain open the entire time you are working in the other application.

Out for Launch If you can't launch the attachment, it's probably because you don't have that application installed on your computer. A little giveaway is the icon representing the attachment. If the icon is plain and gray, there's a good chance that you don't have the application in which the attachment was originally created. You can still use the View option as described in the beginning of this lesson to see the unformatted contents of the attachment.

PRINTING THE ATTACHMENT

Printing the attachment is not a problem when you have the application program installed on your computer. You can print it from that program.

You can still print the attachment if you don't have the application program.

1. Double-click the attachment icon to open the file.
2. Click the View button on the Properties box.
3. Choose File, Print. The File Print dialog box appears (see Figure 13.6).

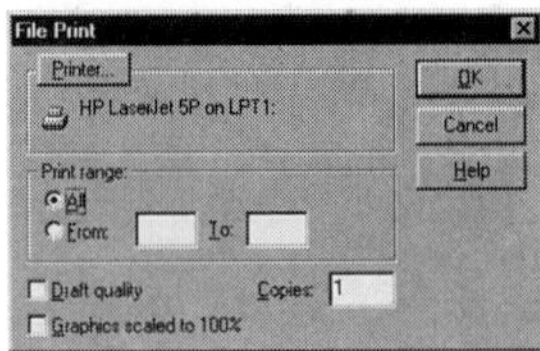

FIGURE 13.6 The File Print dialog box.

4. (Optional) The default setting in the File Print dialog box is to print all of the document. If you only want to print a portion of the attachment, highlight that segment before you choose File, Print. Then after you open the File Print dialog box, choose Selection under Print Range.

5. Click OK to print the document.

There is one more thing to remember when working with attachments. When you *launch* an attachment, Windows creates a temporary file for you to work in. If you look at the title bar of a launched attachment (no matter which application it's in), you see a series of numbers, not the original file name of the attachment sent to you. If you decide to make changes to that file and save it again, you should use the Save As command to give it a name you'll remember. Also, saving changes this way does not affect the original attachment sent to you.

If someone sends you an attachment for you to make changes to and return back to them, first detach the file. Then open it in its original application, make your changes, save the file, and create a new mail message, attaching the changed file to return back to the sender. Send the file back with a slightly modified file name, maybe with an R at the end of the file name so the recipient knows that you have made revisions and doesn't overwrite his original with your revised file.

For files that you'll be editing and returning, you might want to consider linking or embedding as covered in Lesson 15.

In this lesson, you learned how to create, launch, detach, and print attachments. In the next lesson, you learn how to create Lotus Notes links and Pop-Ups.

LESSON 14 UNDERSTANDING LOTUS NOTES LINKS AND POP-UPS

In this lesson, you learn how to create links within Notes to Notes documents, databases, or views. You also learn how to create Pop-Ups.

CREATING DOCUMENT, DATABASE, AND VIEW LINKS

Links are pointers to other documents or other Lotus Notes databases. If want to send a mail message and refer to a page in the Help database, you can create a document link in your mail message. When the recipient receives your mail, he can double-click the Document Link icon and see the page to which you are referring. This saves you from cutting and pasting information into your mail message. You can only create links in the rich text field (the body) of your mail message.

Links work in the same way that hypertext works in the Help database (as you learned in Lesson 5) except that an icon represents the link. There are three *types* of Lotus Notes links that you can create and include in your mail messages or Lotus Notes documents. See Table 14.1.

TABLE 14.1 TYPES OF LINKS

THIS ICON	NAMED	DOES THIS
	Document Link	Connects to another Lotus Notes document. It can be a mail message or a document within an

continues

TABLE 14.1 CONTINUED

THIS ICON	NAMED	DOES THIS
		entirely different database. Double-clicking a document link results in the linked document appearing on the screen.
	Database Link	Connects to another database opened at its default view.
	View Link	Connects to another database view (other than the default view).

It's important to understand that links will only work when they are linked to documents, views, and databases that others have access to. If you link to a document that has been deleted, or to a database not available to or accessible by the person to whom you are sending the link, it simply won't work.

DOCUMENT LINKS

The examples in this lesson create links to the Help database. Be sure to use the server copy of the Help database, not a local copy. If you have access to discussion databases, or other types of Lotus Notes databases, try these exercises using those databases instead of the Help database.

To create a document link:

1. Begin a mail message by filling in the header (address, subject line, and so on) information.
2. In the body field of your message, type a sentence telling the recipient what information your document link contains (this is a courtesy, not a requirement). You might type something such as **I'm learning how to create a document link. If you want to learn how to, click here.**

3. Press the Spacebar at the end of your sentence. Choose Window, Workspace from the menu to return to your workspace area without exiting this mail message.
4. Double-click the Help database icon to open the database. Do a quick search for Doclinks. Double-click to open the Creating a link document.
5. With the Help document open, choose Edit, Copy as Link, Document Link from the menu.
6. You created your document link. The next step is to paste it into your mail message. Choose Window, New Memo from the menu to return to your memo.
7. Place your cursor at the end of your sentence, remembering to leave the blank space. Choose Edit, Paste to insert the Document Link icon into your mail message (see Figure 14.1).
8. Send your mail message. Press Esc to close the Help database.

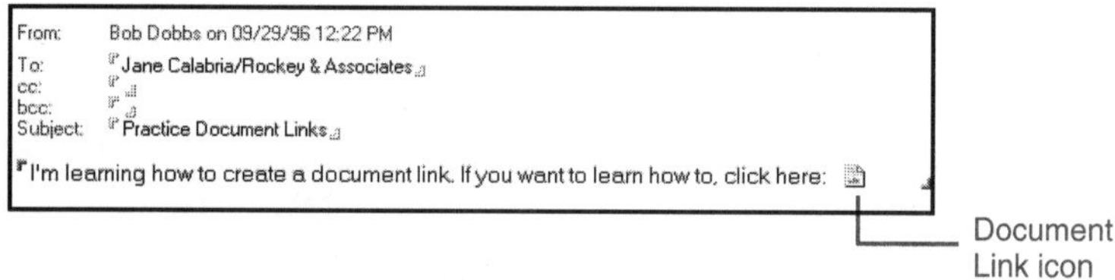

FIGURE 14.1 A document link within a mail message.

You can see the results of your document link by looking at the copy of the mail message you just sent. Open the Sent view of your mailbox and double-click the copy of the mail message you just created. If you want to display the name of the *linked* document, click the document link and hold down your mouse key. The name of the linked document appears as shown in Figure 14.2.

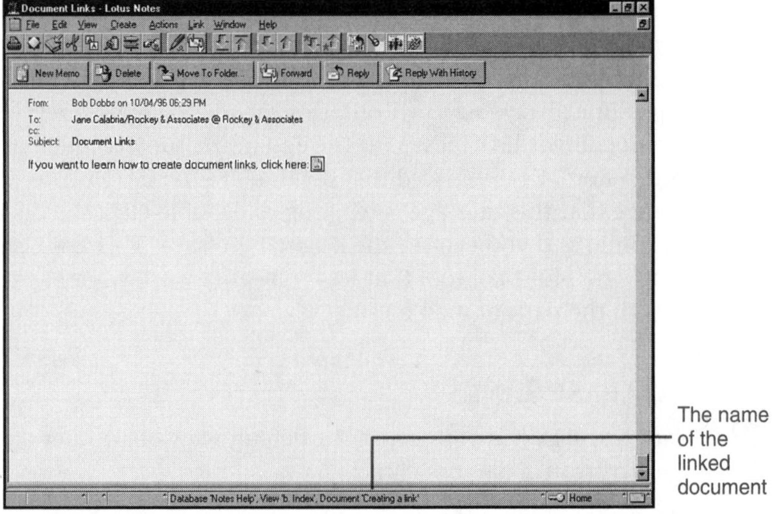

FIGURE 14.2 Click and hold to display the name of the linked document.

If you want to *see* the linked document, double-click the Document Link icon.

A Weak Link? Remember, the success of links is dependent upon the proper rights, or access, to a document or database. Be careful using document links with mail messages. For example, no one has access to your Inbox but you. You won't have success sending a document link to "Bob" so he can see the message you received from "Mary" that is in your Inbox. Bob can't access your mailbox. In this case, you would forward Mary's message to Bob.

Lotus Notes automatically creates document links when you use the *reply* option of Mail. Look in your Inbox and locate a mail message you've received as a reply. It's easy to identify replies; the subject line always starts with R. Double-click to open a reply. You see a document link located at the end of the subject line. Lotus Notes automatically placed that document link; it points to the message that this message is replying to. Double-click the document link, and you can see the original message. This is an extremely helpful Mail tool that lets you easily work your way back through the path of mail messages.

DATABASE LINKS

A *database* link will connect to the default view of another database. To create a database link:

1. Begin a mail message by filling in the header (address, subject line, and so on) information.
2. In the body field of your message, type a sentence telling the recipient what information your document link contains.
3. Press the Spacebar at the end of your sentence. Choose Window, Workspace from the menu to return to your workspace area without exiting this mail message.
4. Click the Help database to select it (it's not necessary to open the database).
5. Choose Edit, Copy as Link, and Database Link from the menu.
6. Choose Window, New Memo from the menu to return to your memo.
7. Place your cursor at the end of your sentence, remembering to leave the blank space. Choose Edit, Paste to insert the Database Link icon into your mail message.
8. Send your message.

You can test this link by looking at your copy of the sent message in Sent mail. When you double-click a database link, it opens the default view of the database.

VIEW LINKS

A *view* link works similar to document links and database links. To create a view link, follow the previous steps, but open the view to which you want to link when you copy your view link. Choose Edit, Copy as Link, View Link as your menu commands.

CREATING POP-UPS

A *Text Pop-Up hotspot* displays pop-up text. This is handy when you send information to several people, and only parts of that information are needed by some of those people. For example, if you're inviting a group to a meeting, and you want to supply directions to the building, a Pop-Up can do the job for you. Some people might not need the directions, others may. By using a Pop-Up, those who need the directions can click a word and additional text appears with directions to that location as seen in Figure 14.3.

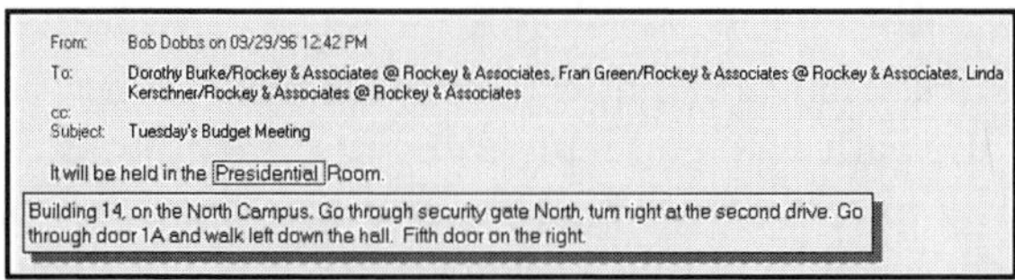

FIGURE 14.3 A Text Pop-Up hotspot.

A Text Pop-Up can only be created in the rich text field (body) of your mail message. To create this kind of hotspot:

1. Begin a mail message by filling in the header information.
2. In the body of the mail message, type your message. Determine which word you would like to become the text hotspot word (Figure 14.3 uses the meeting room name).

3. Highlight that word by selecting it with your mouse. Choose Create, Hotspot, Text Pop-Up from the menu.
4. The Text Pop-up Properties box appears as shown in Figure 14.4.

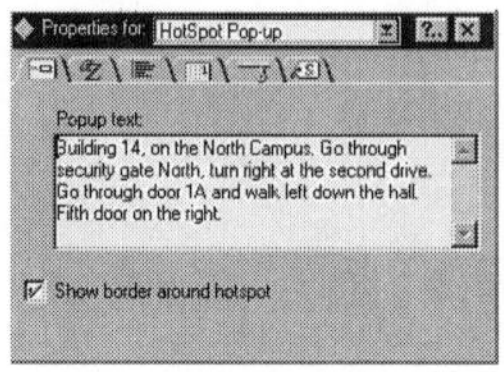

FIGURE 14.4 The Text Pop-up HotSpot Properties box.

5. Fill in the text you want to pop up when this hotspot is clicked.
6. Close the Properties box. Finish and send your message.

You can see the effects of your Pop-Up by looking at the copy of your message in Sent mail.

You can use text Pop-Ups to be humorous or sarcastic within a mail message. The pop-up text can include the "real" meaning behind your typewritten word.

In this lesson, you learned how to create document links and how to follow the path of a mail reply using document links. You also learned how to create text Pop-Ups. In the next lesson, you learn more about linking and how to embed files into your mail message.

LESSON 15

Linking and Embedding

In this lesson, you discover two concepts: linking and embedding. You also learn how to use these concepts in Lotus Notes to work with other applications.

Sharing Information from Other Applications

To exchange information with other Notes Mail users, you can go beyond the capabilities of Notes. You can incorporate data that you created in other applications such as a spreadsheet, a word processing document, a graph, a drawing, or a scanned image. Rather than keying that information into your mail message or faxing a hard copy, you can capture it from the original program and place it in your mail memo. Then all the recipients have the ability to view the data and comment on it.

There are several methods to bring data from other programs into Lotus Notes. You learned about many of those ways in previous lessons. In this lesson, you concentrate on linking and embedding.

You can share information between applications using:

- *Attached files* Allow you to include copies of files in the "native" format of its originating program. (You learned about attached files in Lesson 13).
- *Document Links* Let you include a reference to another Lotus Notes document (see Lesson 14).
- *Importing* Converts data from its "native" program so you can include it in your Notes document. Generally,

users import data when they can't edit or open the source document. Importing is not often used as a Lotus Notes Mail function, but is useful in other Notes databases. The *10 Minute Guide to Lotus Notes 4.5* discusses importing.

- *Edit, Cut and Edit, Copy commands* Allow you to store data temporarily in the Clipboard (a memory-holding area created by Windows or Macintosh) and then place it into your document with the Edit, Paste command. These are standard Windows commands used in almost any Windows-based program.
- *Linking* Utilizes the Clipboard (via the Cut and Copy commands) to bring data from a source document and place it into your document. Any updates to the source information will also appear in your Lotus Notes document. All users of the Notes document must have access to the source file for this to work, and the location of that file cannot change or the link will fail.
- *Embedding* Places an "object" created by another program directly into your document. You can edit the object contents by activating the source application directly from your document. Changing an embedded object does not change the source document.

Dynamic Data Exchange (DDE) is the communications protocol that lets you share data between two *open* applications. DDE is an older technology, so most programs in Windows and OS2 support it.

Object Linking and Embedding (OLE) extends your ability to dynamically share information between programs and program files. Because of OLE, you can embed or link files from another application into a Lotus Notes document; or you can embed a new object and use the object's application to enter data into the Notes document. Not all applications support OLE, so you may not be able to embed files from all of your applications.

Object An *object* is a single piece of data such as text, graphics, sound, rich text, or animation created by an OLE-supportive application.

In DDE/OLE, the "client" application requests data from the "server" (or source) application, incorporates it, and displays the object. The server application updates the object if it is linked. For example, if you want to bring Lotus 1-2-3 spreadsheet information into a Lotus Notes memo, Lotus 1-2-3 is the server application and Lotus Notes is the client application.

As a user, you don't have to know if an application supports DDE or OLE. Lotus Notes automatically employs OLE if the server application supports it and DDE if it doesn't.

UNDERSTANDING LINKING

When you link data from an application to your Lotus Notes document, the linked object maintains a reference or pointer back to the originating file. Then, when the original file changes, the modifications also appear in the Lotus Notes document.

For example, if you copy data from a Lotus 1-2-3 spreadsheet file containing your yearly budget into a Lotus Notes document and link the data to its source, any new data you add to the spreadsheet file at the end of the first quarter will also show up in your Notes document. Likewise, anyone else who also linked data to their own Notes document or who are using your Notes document in a shared database will also receive the updates to the spreadsheet.

As a user, you can't edit or update linked data without using the source application program. You would also need access to the source file and find the file at the same drive and directory or folder as listed in the reference pointer to the source file. In other words, if the file the data came from was on the server's drive F: in the \Import directory, you need to specify F:\Import as the source location and access it from your computer.

What are the advantages of linking files?

- You can link files between older Windows programs that don't support embedding.
- You can change the source file and automatically update any documents linked to it.
- Linked files require less memory than embedded objects.

What are the disadvantages?

- You can't change the location of the source file or delete it entirely because you'll break the link between the documents.
- The linked document must be in a shared location.
- Links that update automatically may slow down operations.

CREATING LINKS

To create a link from a source document to your Lotus Notes document:

1. Open the source file in the server application program.
2. Select the data you want to copy.
3. Choose Edit, Copy to place a copy of the data in the Clipboard.
4. Switch to Lotus Notes.
5. Open the document to which you want to add the linked data and make sure you are in the edit mode.
6. Position your cursor where you want to place the object.
7. Choose Edit, Paste Special. The Paste Special dialog box appears as shown in Figure 15.1.
8. Select Paste link to source.

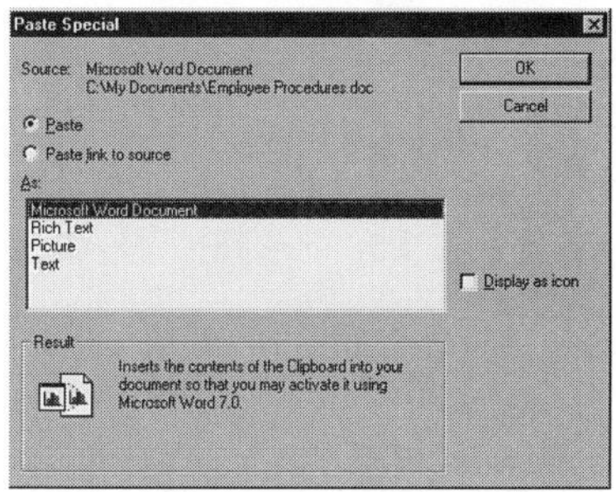

FIGURE 15.1 The Paste Special dialog box.

9. Choose a display format in the As box. The linked object appears in your Notes document, similar to Figure 15.2.

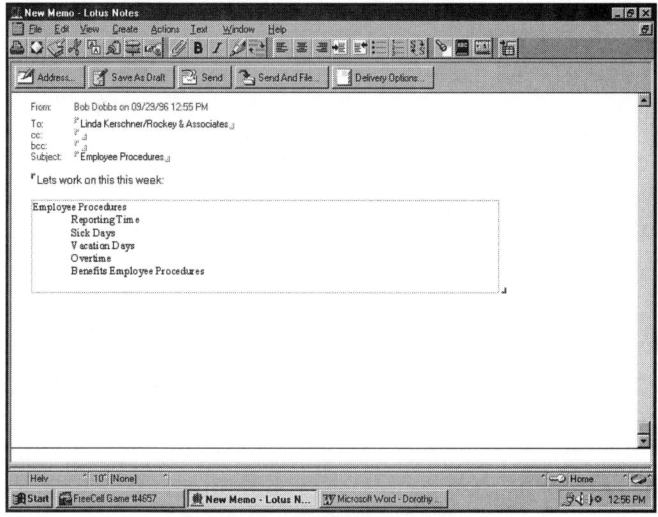

FIGURE 15.2 The linked data shown in the document.

10. (Optional) If you'd rather see an icon in your document instead of the linked data, select Display as icon (see Figure 15.3).

11. Click OK.

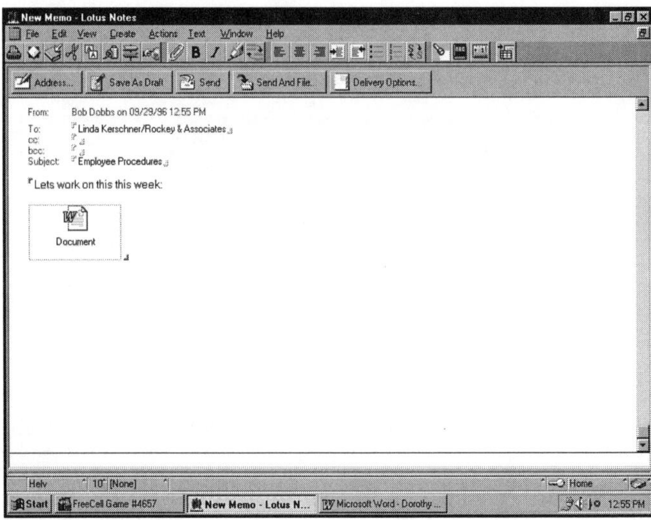

FIGURE 15.3 The data displayed as an icon.

Some applications support the newer OLE 2.0 technology, which lets you link data by using drag-and-drop. To do this, starting in the server (source) application, select the data you want to link, hold down the Control and Shift keys, and drag the selected data to your Lotus Notes document. Release the mouse button to drop the data where you want it to appear in your document.

Once your linked data appears in a document, Lotus Notes tries to update that information each time you open the document. A dialog box appears (see Figure 15.4), asking if you want to refresh the information. Answer Yes or No.

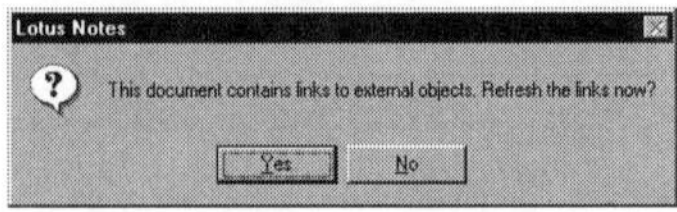

FIGURE 15.4 Dialog box asking if you want to refresh the linked information.

UNDERSTANDING EMBEDDING

When you embed a file or object, a copy appears in the Lotus Notes document. An embedded file maintains no connection to the server (source) application file, so updates to the source file don't change your Notes document.

What are the advantages of embedding?

- Since the Notes document and the data are stored together, you don't need to maintain links, path names, and source files.
- You don't even have to keep the source data because it becomes part of the Notes document.
- To update the embedded object, you can stay right in Lotus Notes. You don't have to go out to the source application.

What are the disadvantages?

- The documents that contain embedded objects are larger than other documents, so they may take longer to send and they take up more storage space.
- If you update an embedded graphic, you may end up with a file that prints at a lower resolution than the original (not as clear a copy).
- The embedded document has no relationship to the original document. You have to update each document individually, instead of updating only the source document.

EMBEDDING OBJECTS

To embed a file in a Lotus Notes document:

1. Open or create the memo where you want to store the embedded file.

2. Make sure your document is in the edit mode, and then position your cursor where you want the object to appear.

3. Choose Create, Object. The Create Object dialog box appears (see Figure 15.5).

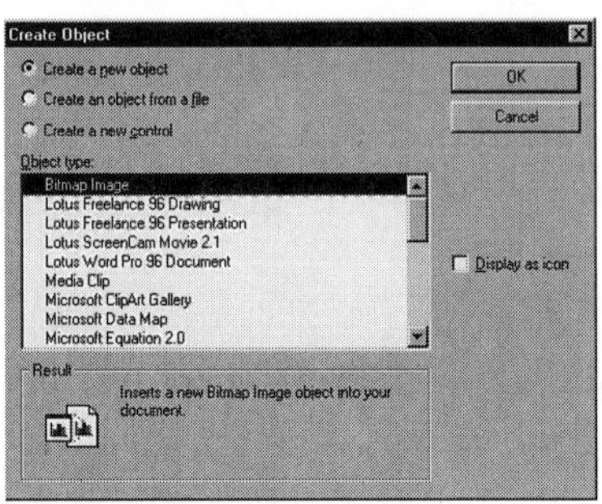

Figure 15.5 The Create Object dialog box.

4. Select Create an object from a file.

5. Under File, enter the file name and path to the file. Click the Browse button to look for this information if you don't know it.

6. If you'd rather display an icon instead of the embedded data, choose Display as icon.

7. Click OK.

Drag-and-Drop Windows 95 users can drag-and-drop a file to embed it in a Lotus Notes document. Choose Start, Programs, Windows Explorer. Locate the file in the Explorer window, drag the file into the Lotus Notes window, and drop it in the Notes document where you want it to appear.

To edit the data in an embedded object, double-click it to open up the file in the source application, as shown in Figure 15.6. Make your changes and click the document outside the embedded object selection border.

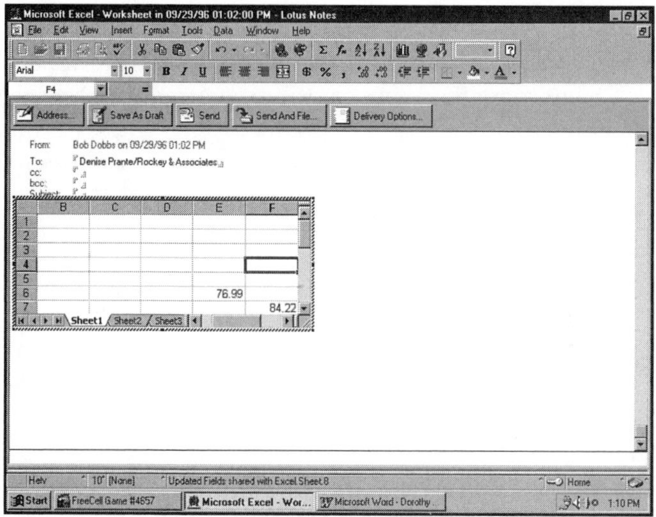

FIGURE 15.6 Editing the embedded object.

You can also paste data to embed it in your document:

1. In the server (source) application, select the data you want.
2. Choose Edit, Copy to copy it to the Clipboard.
3. Switch to Lotus Notes.
4. Open your document in the edit mode, and position your cursor where you want the embedded object to appear.
5. Choose Edit, Paste Special. The Paste Special dialog box appears (see Figure 15.1)
6. Select Paste.
7. From the As box, pick the source from which you copied the data.

8. If you want to display an icon instead of showing the embedded data, choose Display as icon.

9. Click OK.

You can also create and embed new objects in Lotus Notes documents. A blank work file opens for the application you selected, and you enter your data in that work file. When you save your work, it saves as an object in Lotus Notes and not as a separate file.

To create and embed new objects in a Lotus Notes document:

1. In Lotus Notes, open or create the document where you want to place the embedded object. Position your cursor where you want the embedded object to appear.

2. Choose Create, Object. The Create Object dialog box appears (see Figure 15.7).

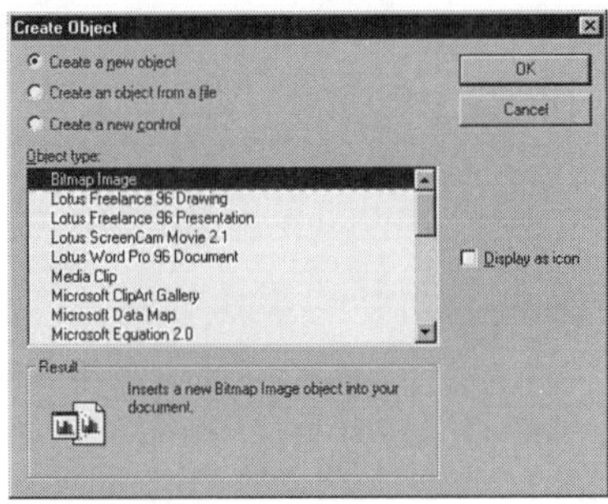

FIGURE 15.7 The Create Object dialog box.

3. Select the Create a new object option.

4. In the Object type list, select the object type that matches the application you want to use.

5. (Optional) If you want to display an icon instead of the embedded data, choose Display as icon.

6. Click OK.

7. Enter data in the blank work file (see Figure 15.8).
8. There are several ways to save and exit the new object and return to your Notes document, depending on the source application that you used to create the object. Choose one of the following methods:
    - Select File, Update.
    - Select File, Update Lotus Notes.
    - Select File, Exit & Return to Lotus Notes.
    - Click the document outside the embedded object border.

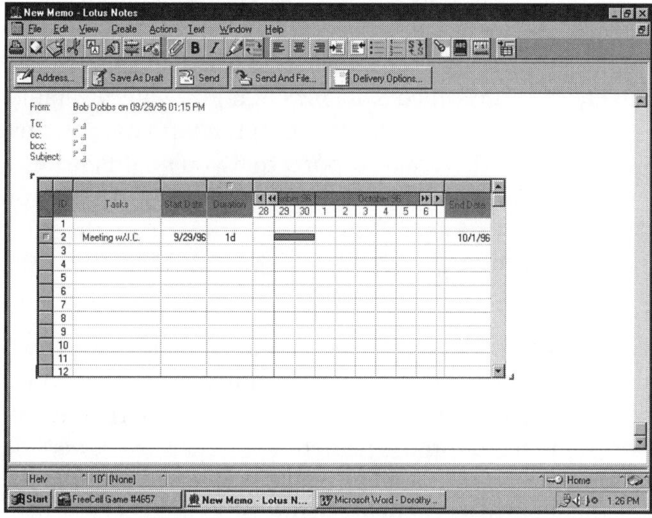

FIGURE 15.8 Entering data into a blank work file.

In this lesson, you learned about linking and embedding and how to place linked data and embedded objects in Lotus Notes documents. In the next lesson, you learn about using Mail tools.

LESSON 16

Using Mail Tools

In this lesson, you learn how to create stationery, select letterhead, and activate an Out of Office Message. You also learn how to send a phone message and a serial route message.

Creating Stationery

You can create forms called *Stationery* that give you the ability to reuse the form and the recipients list on the form over and over again. This is good for weekly reports that you might create through Lotus Notes Mail. You store stationery forms that you create in your Drafts folder. When you want to reuse the stationery form, open the form from Drafts. You may have several stationery forms.

Lotus Notes uses a template to build your stationery. The two default templates are: Memo, which is the Mail Message form, and Personal Stationery, which contains two more rich text fields than the Mail Memo form. One rich text field is at the very beginning of the form, before the From field, the other, at the very end of the form after the body field. Figure 16.1 shows a Personal Stationery form using these two fields to add information about the form. Since these are rich text fields, you are free to include graphics, links, attachments, and so on in these fields.

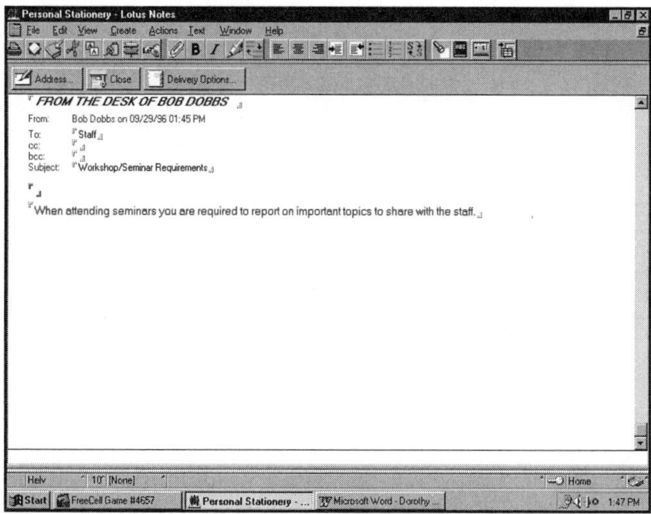

FIGURE 16.1 The Personal Stationery template.

To create stationery:

1. Open your Mail database and choose Actions, Mail Tools, Create Stationery from the menu.
2. In the Create Stationery dialog box (see Figure 16.2), select which template you want to use, the Memo or Personal Stationery template. Click OK.
3. Fill in the To: field, and any other fields and text you want to appear each time you use this form.
4. If you want this message to be delivered with options other than the defaults (maybe you want to attach a Mood Stamp, or make this a high priority delivery), click the Delivery Options button on the Action bar to set your preferences.

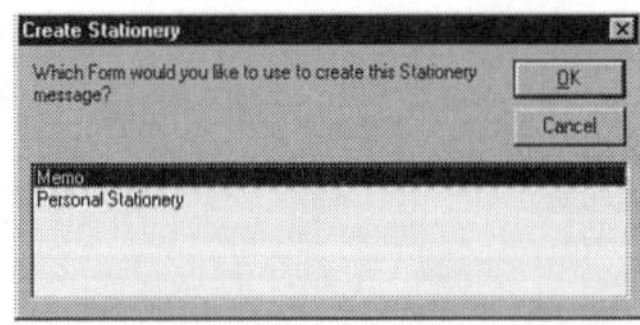

FIGURE 16.2 The Create Stationery dialog box.

5. Click the Close button on the Action bar. You'll be asked if you want to save this as stationery, choose Yes. A confirmation message as shown in Figure 16.3 will appear.
6. Click OK to save and close the form.

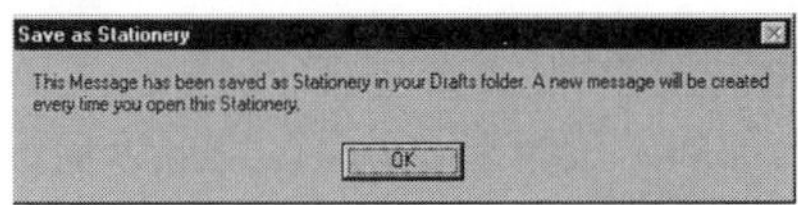

FIGURE 16.3 The Save as Stationery confirmation dialog box.

The body of both templates, the Memo and the Personal Stationery templates, is the same body field as the Mail Message template. This is a rich text field. Figure 16.4 shows this field used to insert a table for a weekly sales report. This example uses the Personal Stationery template with centered, bolded, and blue text in those fields, and a table in the body field for recipients to supply sales call information. With this kind of "design" leverage, you can use your stationery forms for lots of information such as weekly expense or sales reports. You can even link or embed information in the rich text fields as discussed in Lesson 15.

You can delete your stationery by selecting it in your Drafts view, and pressing the Del key.

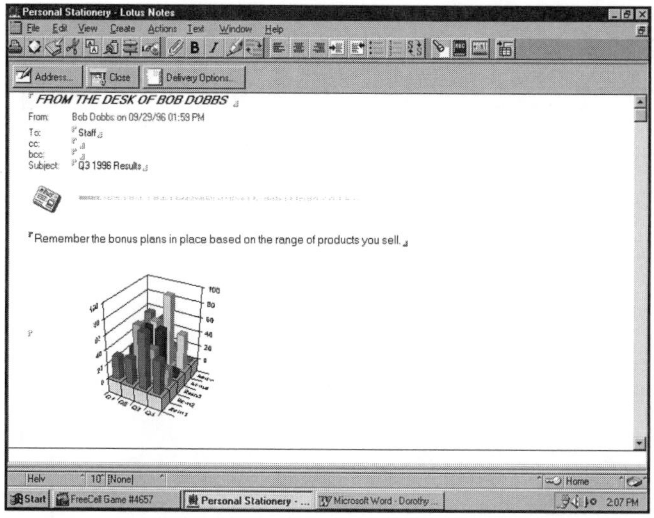

FIGURE 16.4 Personal Stationery created with a table in the body field.

CHOOSING LETTERHEAD

Letterhead allows you to pick a template that contains graphics and becomes your default Mail Message form. Once you pick which letterhead you want, you can change it at any time. If you select a letterhead, the letterhead is the form used when you create stationery and use the Memo template as described in the previous section.

To select letterhead:

1. Open your Mail database. Choose Actions, Mail Tools, and Select Letterhead.
2. The Choose Letterhead dialog box appears as shown in Figure 16.5, scroll through the list to see which letterhead you want to use. The letterhead appears on your screen as you scroll through the list.

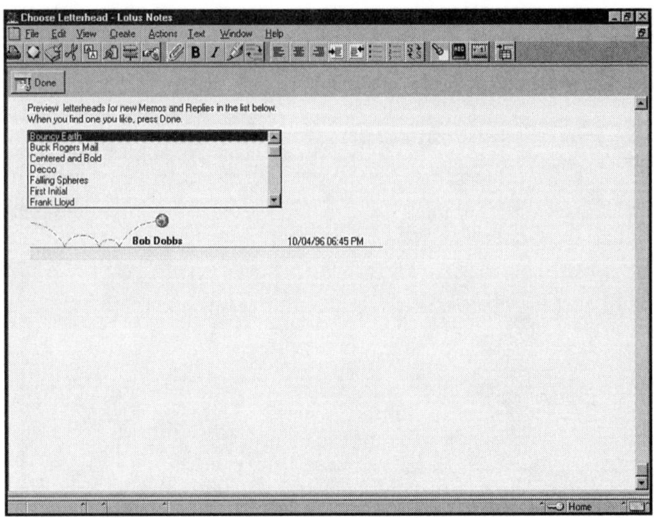

FIGURE 16.5 The Choose Letterhead dialog box.

3. When you find the letterhead you like, click the Done button on the Action bar.
4. Create a new mail message to see your new letterhead in use.

To change your letterhead, follow steps 1 through 4 for selecting letterhead.

If you want to go back to the original Mail Message form with no letterhead, follow steps 1 through 4 and select Plain Text as the type of letterhead, the first choice on the list of available letterheads.

USING THE OUT OF OFFICE MESSAGE

The Out of Office message allows you to respond to incoming mail messages while you are away from the office. You can create a standard message that will be automatically sent as responses to incoming messages so that people know you are away. This is a good tool for times that you will be away from the office for long periods of time, such as vacations, and will not have access to your mail.

You can also create a separate message for a special group of people, who may need some additional information during your absence. For example, you can send a unique message to a special committee or workgroup in which someone else will be handling your responsibilities while you're gone. You can add any special instructions or contact information into that message.

To create an Out of Office message:

1. Open your Mail database. Choose Actions, Mail Tools, and Out of Office from the menu.
2. The Out of Office Profile form appears. There are four sections to this form. In the first section, add the dates for Leaving and Returning. Figure 16.6 shows those fields.

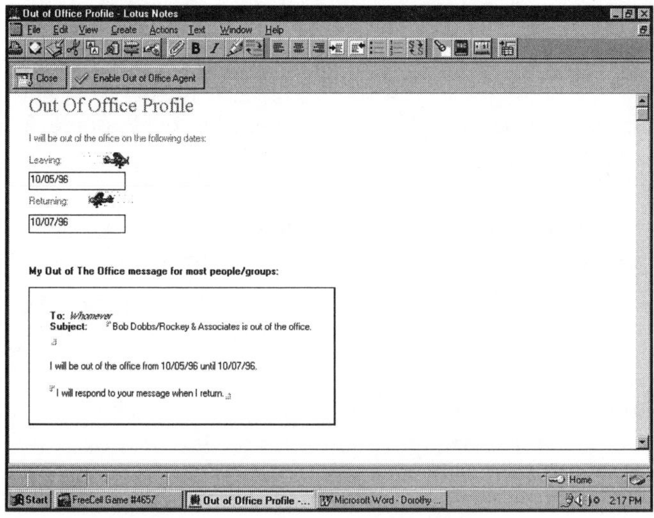

FIGURE 16.6 Out of Office Profile form with Leaving and Returning dates.

3. The second section provides a place for you to type your Out of Office message that will be delivered to "most" people. This will actually be delivered to all people, unless you indicate otherwise in sections 3 and 4. Type your message in this section. Figure 16.7 Shows this section.

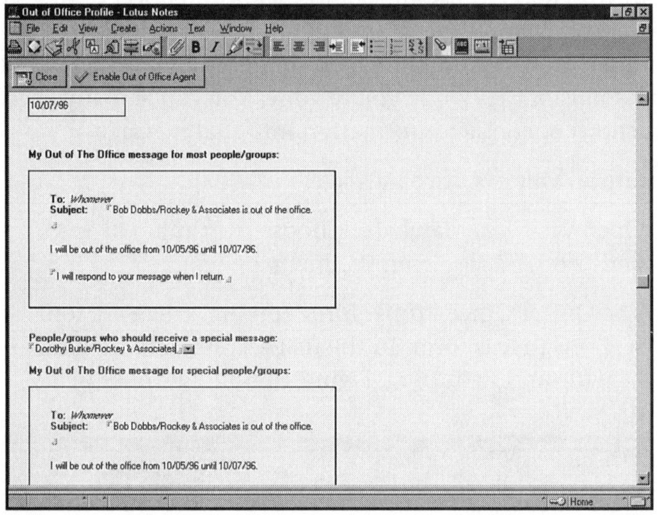

FIGURE 16.7 The Out of Office message for most people. This is your default message.

4. (Optional) Section 3 enables you to provide a message for a special person or a group of people. To select people for this group, press the down arrow key. When the dialog box appears, select people from your address book. Figure 16.8 shows people selected for this group.

5. Type your special message in the My Out of The Office message for special people/groups section as shown in Figure 16.8.

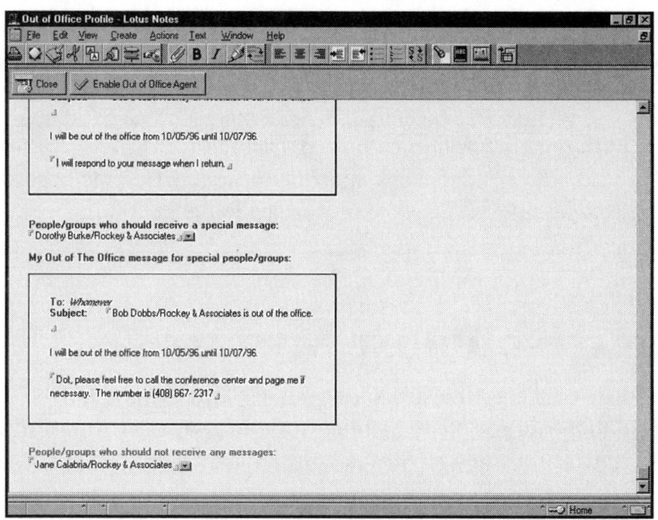

FIGURE 16.8 People selected for a special message.

6. The fourth section allows you to list people who should not receive any notification at all. Click the drop-down arrow key and select people or groups for this field, or you can leave it blank.

7. Click the Enable Out of Office Agent button on the Action bar. A dialog box confirms that the agent is enabled. Click the OK button.

When you return to the office, you need to disable the Out of Office Message. If you return on the date that you indicated in the Out of Office Profile form, you need to do nothing. If you return early, you need to disable the Out of Office message:

1. Open your Mail database. Choose Actions, Mail Tools, and Out of Office from the menu.

2. When the Out of Office Profile form appears, click the I have returned to the office button located on the Action bar.

Don't Forget to Replicate! If you are a remote user and you have created an Out Of Office message from your remote PC, be certain to replicate your Mail database before leaving for your trip. Otherwise, the server will not be notified that this agent needs to run. Refer to Lessons 23 through 26 for remote user information.

CREATING PHONE MESSAGES

In addition to creating tasks for yourself and others, Lotus Notes gives you a tool for creating telephone message information and mailing that message to others who are using Lotus Notes Mail.

Phone messages are straightforward. When you create a phone message, you are filling in a Notes form, in this case, the Phone Message form. It works in the same way that you fill out a mail message since the Phone Message forms are *mail enabled.* This means that when you complete the form, you click the Send button on the Action bar and the message will be mailed to the person or persons in the To:, cc:, and bcc: fields.

To create a phone message:

1. Open your Mail database, or click the Mail database icon once to select it.
2. Choose Create, Special, and Phone Message from the menu.
3. The Phone Message form appears as shown in Figure 16.9. Fill in the To: field and any other information you want to supply with this message.
4. Use the rich text field, Message to type any additional information that the caller supplied with his message.
5. Click the Send button on the Action bar to send the message.

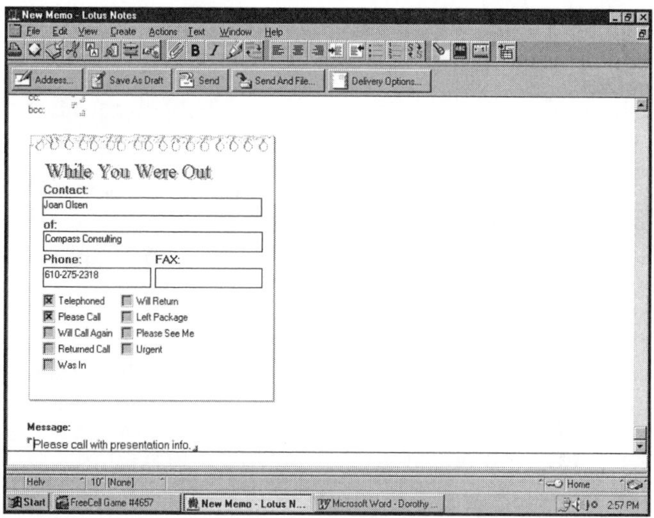

FIGURE 16.9 The Phone Message form completed and ready to send.

CREATING SERIAL ROUTE MESSAGES

Within Mail, you also have the ability to route messages. Different than a distribution list, or a list of names in the To:, cc:, and bcc: fields, routing a message means that it will go to people in the order that you list them. For example, if you are mailing expense reports through Lotus Notes Mail, either by attaching, copying and pasting, or embedding them, serial routing gives you the ability to submit the report first to your manager, then to their manager, and then to the accounting department.

However, you don't have to be using expense reports to appreciate serial routing. You might have a mail memo that you want delivered to people in a certain order. For these purposes, serial mail routing is the way to go.

A Serial Route message will be routed to each person listed in the Route to: field of the memo in the order in which you place people's names. You can address this memo to a list of individuals only; you can't use groups that you created in your address book. To create a Serial Route message:

1. Open your Mail database, or select it in your workspace by clicking the Mail database icon.
2. Choose Create, Special, and Serial Route Memo from the menu.
3. The Serial Route Memo does not have a cc: or bcc: field. Fill in the Route To field with the names of those you want to route. Put them in the order that you want to route them.
4. If you want to be notified of the delivery of this message to each recipient as they receive it, click the Notify Sender at Each Stop box.
5. Click the Send button in the Action bar to send this message.

In this lesson, you learned how to create and customize stationery and select letterhead. You also learned how to create, enable, and disable an Out of Office message. In the next lesson, you'll learn how to use Lotus Notes workflow options.

LESSON 17

Using Workflow Options

In this lesson, you learn about using Lotus Notes Mail to assign and follow the workflow of your projects. Lotus Notes helps you keep track of your personal To Do list, as well as record the tasks that you have assigned to others. You can check the status of the these tasks, keeping on top of any projects you manage.

Assigning Tasks

To keep track of all the things you have to do, you can assign tasks to yourself. For example, if you know you have a presentation to give in two weeks, you can assign a task to yourself noting all the things you must prepare for that date.

1. Open your Mail database. Choose Create, Task from the menu. The New Task form appears as shown in Figure 17.1.
2. Enter a description of the task under Task.
3. To set a priority for the task, click High, Medium, or Low (the default is None).
4. Enter a date in the Due box to set a due date for the task.
5. To establish a start date for the task, enter the date in the Start box.
6. (Optional) In Additional information, add any information you want explaining the task or how it is to be completed.

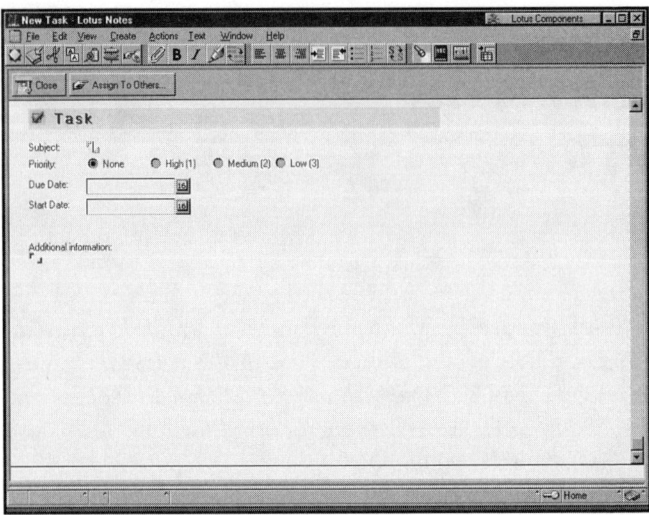

FIGURE 17.1 The New Task form.

7. Click the Close button on the Action bar.
8. When the alert box appears asking if you want to save the document, choose Yes.
9. The task appears in the To Do view of the Mail Navigator pane (see Figure 17.2).

If other people are involved in a project with you, you can also assign tasks to them. For instance, you and your staff may plan to attend your annual convention in three weeks. You want each member of the staff to know his or her areas of responsibility, such as reserving rooms and flights, packing and sending materials for the exhibit booth, arranging for rentals of audio visual equipment, or preparing presentations for seminars you are offering at the convention. You can create tasks for each member of your staff and set due dates.

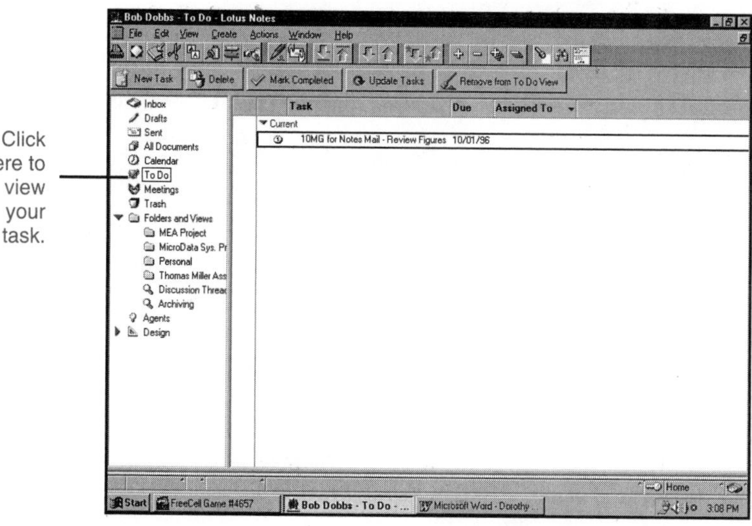

FIGURE 17.2 The To Do view of the Mail database.

1. Follow steps 1 through 5 of assigning a task to yourself.
2. Click the Assign to Others button on the Action bar. Two new fields appear on the form (see Figure 17.3).
3. In the Assign to field, enter the name of the person to whom you are assigning the task.
4. Put the names of anyone who should receive a copy of this task in the cc: field.
5. In Additional information, add any information you want explaining the task or how it is to be completed.
6. Click the Send button on the Action bar (click Close instead, if you want to save the task without sending it).

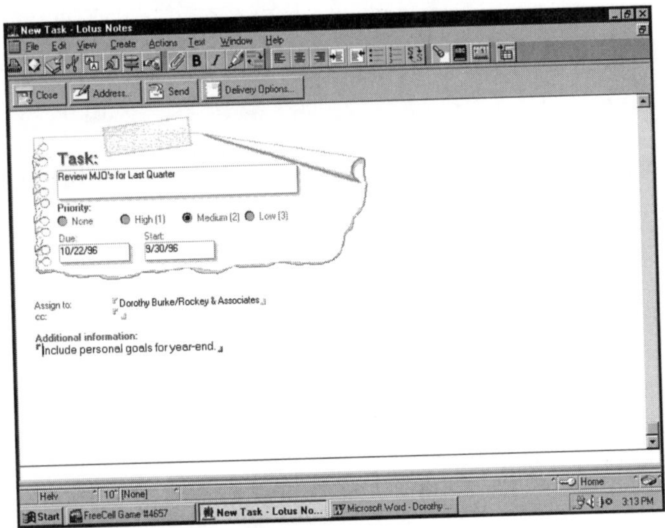

FIGURE 17.3 A task assigned to others.

CONVERTING MAIL TO TASKS

Quite frequently, you will receive mail messages requesting that you do something. You can convert these messages into tasks, so they will appear on your To Do list. For example, if you get a mail message from your manager asking you to prepare your department's budget for next year and have it to him by the end of the month, you can add that to the To Do view so you won't forget to work on it.

1. Select the document in the View pane or open the message.
2. Choose Actions, Convert to Task.
3. The mail message appears as a Task document, and you can make any changes or additions you want to the information provided there.

4. If you want to assign the task to yourself, click the Close button on the Action bar, or press the Esc key.

   To assign the task to anyone else, click the Assign to Others button on the Action bar, fill in the Assign to and cc: fields, and then click the Send button on the Action bar.

Viewing Task Status

To keep track of the tasks you assign to yourself, tasks others assign to you, and tasks you assign to others, open the To Do view in the Mail database.

The To Do view divides the tasks into Completed, Current, Future, Overdue, and Today categories. It also displays messages that ask you to respond by a particular date.

To remove a message from the To Do view, select it, and click the Remove from To Do View button on the Action bar. Although this removes the message from the To Do view, it doesn't delete it from the Mail database.

Marking a Completed Task

When a task is completed, you need to mark it so you know it's done. Marking it completed moves the task into the Complete category of the To Do view. If someone else assigned the task to you, that person gets a message showing that you completed the task. A copy of that message appears under the task in your To Do view.

To mark a task as completed:

1. From the To Do view, select or open the task.
2. Click the Mark Completed button on the Action bar. The task moves under the Completed area in the To Do view (see Figure 17.4).

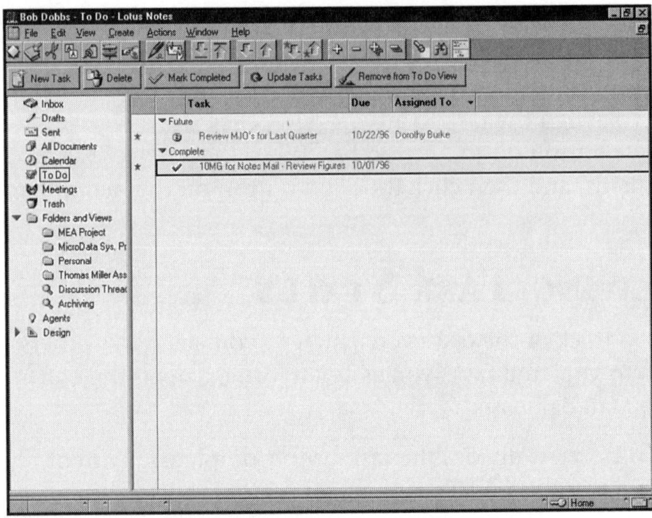

FIGURE 17.4 A completed task.

If you opened the task in order to mark it completed, you will get a prompt asking if you want to send additional comments to the person who assigned the task to you. If you select No, the task will be marked completed. If you select Yes, a mail memo will appear addressed to the person who assigned the task. Complete the mail memo and click the Send button.

UPDATING STATUS

Once a task is created, Notes does not read the task and check the dates constantly. In order for a task to move from the Current category to the Overdue category, you must update the status manually or automatically.

The manual method:

1. Open your Mail database in the To Do view.
2. Click the Update Tasks button on the Action bar.

Notes will read the dates of the tasks and recategorize them if necessary.

The automatic method:

1. Open the Agents view of your Mail database. (See Figure 17.5.)

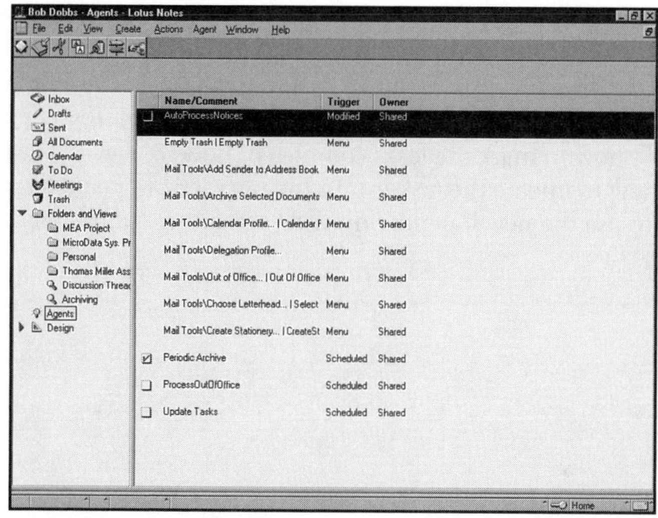

FIGURE 17.5 The Agents view.

What's an Agent? An *agent* is a preset, automatic task, similar to a macro in other programs.

2. Check the box in front of Update Tasks.

Which Server? You may be asked on which server you want the agent to run. If your mail is stored on the Notes server, choose your Mail server; you may not have access to run an agent on that server, so check with your Notes administrator before doing this.

3. Lotus Notes schedules the Update Tasks agent to run each night at 1:00 A.M., unless you change the time.

In this lesson, you learned how to assign tasks to yourself and to others, how to mark the tasks completed, how to view the tasks, and how to update the task list. In the next lesson, you'll learn how to use the new Calendaring and Scheduling features of Notes.

LESSON 18

Setting Up for Calendaring and Scheduling

In this lesson, you learn how to use the new Calendaring and Scheduling features of Notes. You'll also learn how to keep track of your own appointment schedule and allow others to see your free time.

Configuring Options

Group calendaring and scheduling allows you to keep track of your time, check availability of other Notes users and easily see a list of meeting invitations sent to you. Your calendar is part of your Mail database. With the calendar features you can:

- Make appointments on your personal calendar.
- View your calendar in two days, one week, two weeks or one month views.
- Schedule meetings (called "appointments") and invite others.
- View the free time of other Notes users.
- Enter repeating or multi-day appointments (such as monthly meetings or vacations).
- Create a reminder to yourself that will appear in your calendar.

- Enter anniversary information (appointments which repeat weekly, month, yearly and so on).
- Schedule rooms and resources for your meeting.

Your calendar and the information it contains are stored and viewed in your Mail database. Two views are available for scheduling information. They are:

- The Calendar view: Displays appointments you make and meeting information for meetings you have accepted, in a two day, one week, two week or one month format (see Figure 18.1).

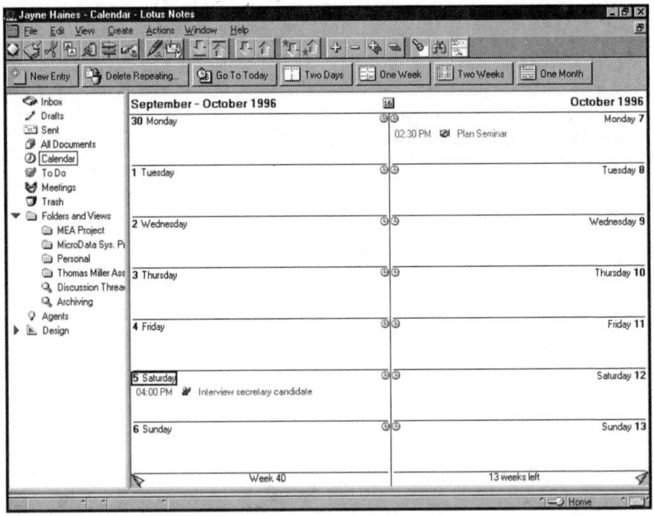

FIGURE 18.1 The Calendar view in the Two Weeks format.

- The Meetings view: Lists meeting invitations and meetings you have accepted by date and meeting time (see Figure 18.2).

Two documents in your Mail database allow you to administer your calendaring and scheduling functions and to determine

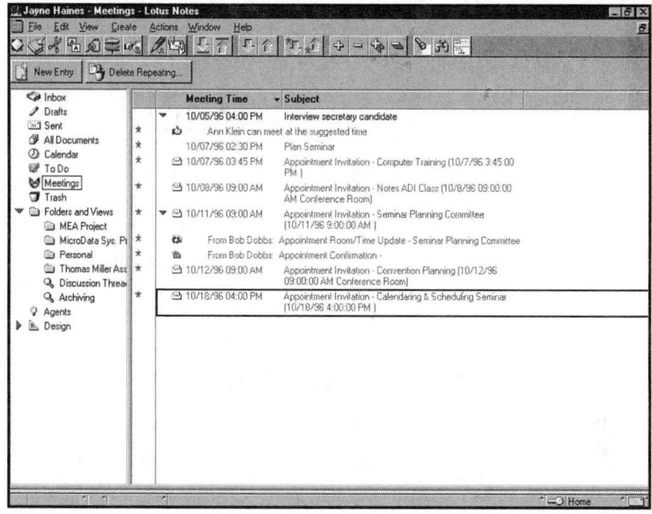

FIGURE 18.2 The Meeting view.

what calendar and mail information you wish to share with others. They are the *Calendar Profile* and the *Delegation Profile*. Table 18.1 describes the sharing options you can select.

TABLE 18.1 HOW YOU CAN SHARE CALENDAR AND MAIL INFORMATION:

IN THE CALENDAR PROFILE, ENTER WHO CAN:	IN THE DELEGATION PROFILE, ENTER WHO CAN:
See your free time	Read your calendar
	Manage your calendar
	Read your mail
	Read and send mail on your behalf
	Read, send, and edit any document in your mail file

continues

TABLE 18.1 CONTINUED

IN THE CALENDAR PROFILE, ENTER WHO CAN:	IN THE DELEGATION PROFILE, ENTER WHO CAN:
	Delete mail in your mail database
	Automatically schedule you for meetings.

SETTING YOUR CALENDAR PROFILE

The Calendar Profile document must be completed before you can begin working with your calendar. Your Notes administrator may have taken this step for you. If you click on your Calendar view and receive a message that your Profile must be set, follow the steps below. Or simply follow the steps below to confirm the information contained in your Calendar Profile document. (See Figure 18.3.)

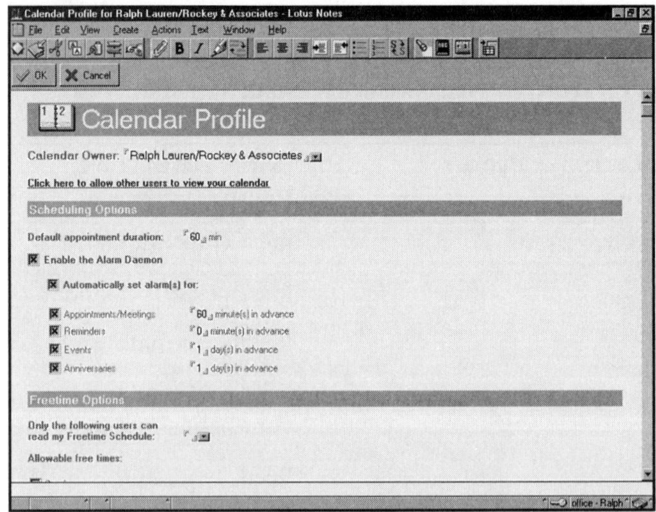

FIGURE 18.3 The Calendar Profile document.

Check with your Notes administrator to confirm that the information you enter in the Calendar Profile and the Delegation Profile agree with your Notes setup at work.

To configure the Calendar Profile:

1. From the workspace, select your Mail database.
2. Choose Actions, Calendar Tools, Calendar Profile from the menu.
3. Confirm that your name appears in the Calendar Owner field.
4. If you wish to allow others to see your calendar, click here and open the Delegation Profile document. (This document is explained in the next section. If you want to allow others to view your calendar, stop here, go to the instructions for the Delegation Profile and return to step 5 below.) If you do not wish others to have access to your calendar, go to step 5 now.

Let Others See My Calendar? No way! Allowing others to see your calendar is very different than allowing others to see your free time. Be careful with this selection. If you allow others to see your calendar, they will see appointments you've entered into your calendar, except for those you specifically mark as "Not for public viewing." Also note that viewing your calendar is not the same as viewing your mail, even though the Calendar view is found in the Mail database. You can also give people access to your mail. See "Setting Your Delegation Profile" in this lesson.

5. In the Scheduling Options portion of this document, enter your Default appointment duration. This is the number of minutes you want between each appointment on your calendar. The default setting is 60 minutes. (See Figure 18.3.)

6. Check the Enable the Alarm Daemon option if you wish to be alerted to upcoming events, appointments, meetings, and so on.

7. Check the Automatically set alarm(s) for option and check Appointments/Meetings, Reminders, Events, or Anniversaries to select which you wish to receive notification of. Also enter the amount of advance notice you want.

8. To restrict access to your free time (see Figure 18.4), click the down arrow next to the Only the following users can read my Freetime Schedule field and add only the names of people who you want to see your free time. Leaving this field blank will allow all Notes users on your server to see your free time. (The purpose of group scheduling is to allow others to see your free time. It is suggested that you leave this field blank.)

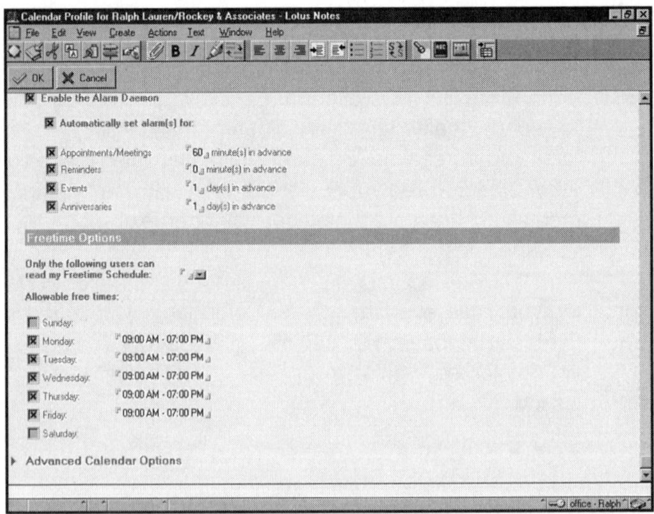

FIGURE 18.4 Scroll down the Calendar Profile to view Freetime Options.

Revealing Your Free Time You can select from the Personal or Public Address Books when entering names of those who you want to see your free time.

9. Enter your Allowable free times. Check the days you are available for scheduling, and enter your available hours for each of the days you selected (the default setting is 9:00 AM to 5:00 PM).

Under the Advanced Calendar Options section (see Figure 18.5), you see a subsection called Autoprocessing Options. Selecting Autopro-cessing options instructs Notes to automatically add information to your calendar. Fill in the following options you desire:

- *Meetings*. Meeting invitations will be automatically accepted and added to your calendar when you select this option, but only if the invitation is sent by those you specified in the field called Autoprocess Meetings only from the following people. Enter names into this field by typing the names or selecting them from the Names dialog box, which is a list of people in your Personal Address Book or the Public Address Book.
- *Remove invitations from my Inbox after I respond to them.* Check this box to delete meeting invitations from the Inbox view once you have accepted or rejected the invitation.
- *Default settings*. Select the Calendar entry type you want to automatically appear when you are making entries.
- *Hide new calendar entries from public viewing*. Check to prevent everyone else from seeing your new entries.
- *Enable conflict checking for*. Select the items you don't want to be in conflict to have Notes check that they don't overlap.

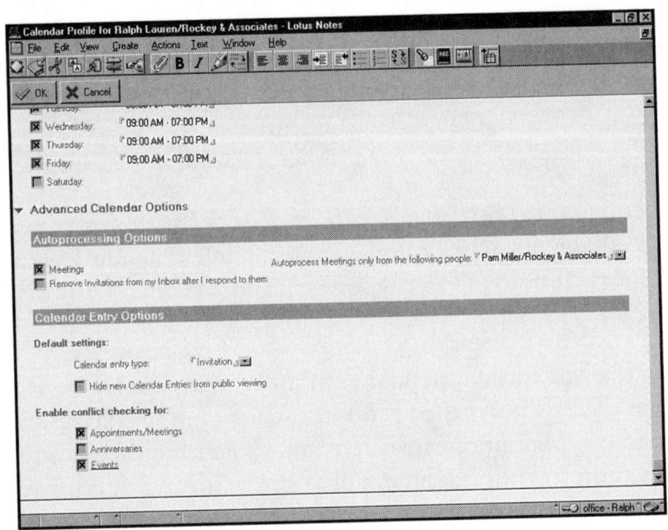

FIGURE 18.5 The Advanced Calendar Options.

When you have completed the information, save the Delegation Profile document by clicking OK on the Action bar or Cancel to exit the document without saving it.

SETTING YOUR DELEGATION PROFILE

The Delegation Profile lets you specify who may view your calendar and who may make entries for you. You can also use this document to designate who may read your mail or send mail on your behalf.

To create a Delegation Profile document (see Figure 18.6), choose Actions, Mail Tools, Delegation Profile from the menu or click the Click here button to allow other users to view your calendar in the Calendar Profile document.

Complete the appropriate fields in the Delegation Profile:

- *Everyone can read my Calendar*. Check this only if you mean it! Checking this field allows access to your calendar by every Notes user on your server. Leave this field without a check mark, and if you wish, enter the names

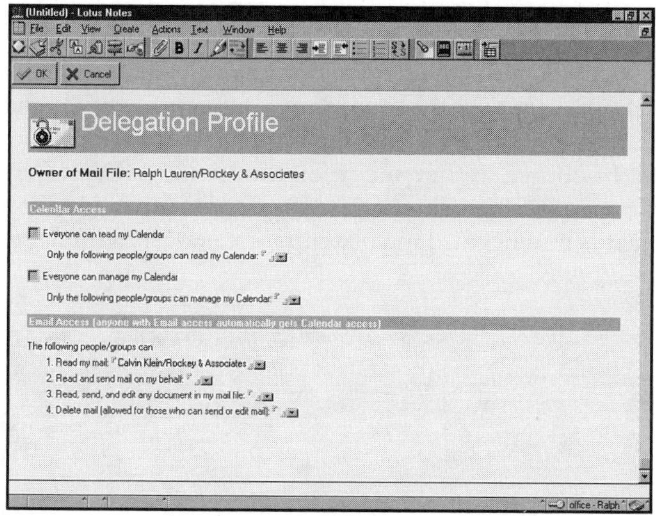

FIGURE 18.6 A Delegation Profile document.

of those people who can view your calendar in Only the following people/groups can read my Calendar.

- *Everyone can manage my Calendar.* Check this only if you mean it! Checking this field gives the rights to change your calendar to every Notes user on your server. To restrict who can manage your calendar, leave this field without a check mark, and enter the names of the people who can modify your calendar entries in Only the following people/groups can manage my Calendar.

In the E-mail Access section of the form, you can specify who can read your mail; read and send mail on your behalf; read, send, and edit documents in your mail database; or delete your mail. Enter or select names in the appropriate fields to grant this permission.

When you are ready, save the Delegation Profile document by clicking OK on the Action bar or Cancel to exit the document without saving it.

CHANGING CALENDAR VIEW OPTIONS

To change your Calendar view options, open your Mail database and select Calendar in the Navigator, so you are in the Calendar view. Then choose View, Calendar from the menu bar. Figure 18.7 shows the options as they appear on the menu bar. Try different views to see which you prefer. Use the Go To option and enter a date that is not included in your current view (for example, June 16, 1998).

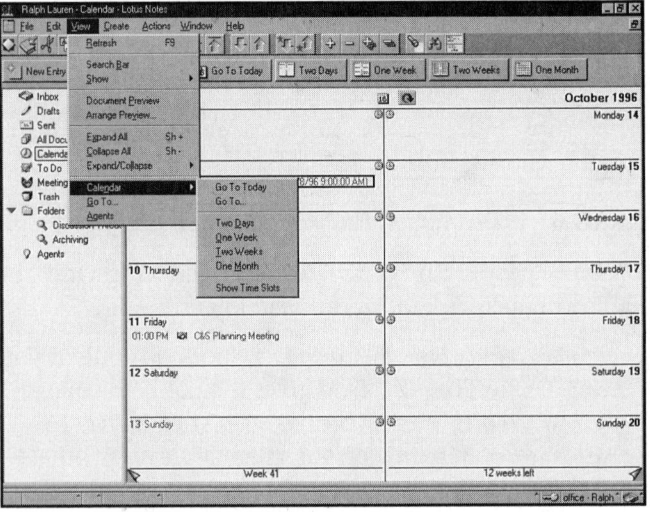

FIGURE 18.7 View, Calendar options.

You can turn a page of the calendar by clicking on the curled page at the bottom of your calendar. Click the curl on the left page to go back in time; click the curl on the right page to go forward.

In this lesson, you learned how to configure your Calendar and Delegation preferences for your mail and your calendar. In the next lesson, you learn how to make appointments and invite others to meetings.

LESSON 19

USING THE CALENDAR

In this lesson you learn how to make entries in your calendar. You also learn how to accept meeting invitations and how to check the available time of others.

MAKING CALENDAR ENTRIES

Entries that you make in your calendar will affect your free time availability. Although others may not be able to view your calendar, they may be able to view your free time. Check with your Notes administrator if you are having difficulty seeing the free time of others. There are several types of calendar entries you can create:

- **Appointment** is a meeting with a non-Notes user, such as a client, or a personal appointment such as a doctor's visit. You cannot invite others to an appointment. You can enter an appointment as one time value, and it can occur once, or repeat.
- **Invitation** is an appointment in which you want to include and invite others. Those you invite must be part of your Notes Mail system and Notes will automatically notify them for you by sending them an invitation in their mail. It is possible that you may also find cc: Mail users and Office Vision users in your Invitation list if your systems administrator configured Lotus Notes to include them.
- **Event** has a duration that lasts for more than one day such as a vacation. Events can occur for a number of consecutive days, or they can be repeated (see Repeat, later in this lesson for more information).

- **Reminder** is a note to yourself which will display on your calendar in the time and date you assign to it.
- **Anniversary** is a repeating occasion that you wish to appear on your calendar weekly, monthly, or yearly.

You can create a calendar entry at any time while in Lotus Notes and you don't have to have the Mail database open. To create a calendar entry:

From anywhere in Notes Select Create, Calendar Entry from the menu.

From your Calendar view in Mail Choose New Entry on the Action bar or double-click on a date or time slot in the calendar.

Follow these instructions to complete the calendar entry:

1. Select the type of appointment you want to create: Appointment, Invitation, Event, Reminder, or Anniversary. Depending upon the type of calendar entry you choose, the entry fields will vary slightly (see Figure 19.1).

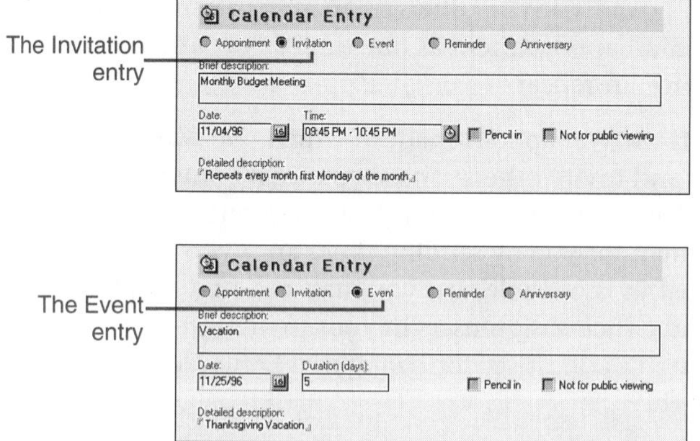

FIGURE 19.1 The fields will vary depending on the calendar entry you choose.

2. Enter information in the the fields in the document. (The remaining fields on the document will vary slightly depending upon the type of entry you have selected):

   Date. Enter the date or click on the Calendar button to see a miniature calendar. Use the left and right arrows at the top of the calendar to move from month to month. Click on the day to select the date. Figure 19.2 shows the miniature calendar.

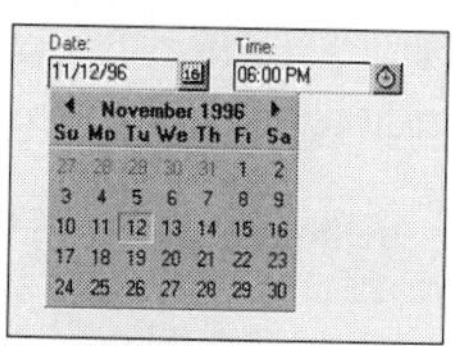

FIGURE 19.2 Choosing a date.

   Time (does not appear for Anniversary or Event). Enter the time or click on the Clock button to see a time scale. Drag the indicators up or down on the scale to set the time and duration of the appointment.

   Duration (appears only for Event). Enter the number of days the event will last.

   Description. Enter a brief description of the appointment.

   Reservations (appears only for Invitation). Three options appear in the Reservations section: You can reserve any available room, a specific room, or resources such as a projector or computer. These options may not be enabled in your company. You should speak with your Notes administrator regarding this section of the form.

   Pencil in marks the entry on your calendar, but does not affect your free time.

   Not for public viewing prevents others from seeing this appointment. Use this if you want to enter a confidential or personal appointment, such as a doctor's visit. Others can see that your line is blocked out but will not see the actual appointment.

3. Use the *Repeat* button on the Action bar for appointments that will occur on more than one date such as a monthly meeting. In the Repeat Rules dialog box, select the Repeat interval from the drop-down list. Based on that choice, set the specifics of the frequency and intervals. Then set the Starting Date. Choose Until and set the ending date or For, and set the length of time. Click OK.
4. Click on the Alarm options button on the Action bar to receive a reminder of this entry. In the Alarm dialog box, specify the number of Minutes, choose Before or After, and enter an Alarm Message. Click on OK.

   If you set a default appointment alarm in the Calendar profile and don't want an alarm for this appointment, check Turn Alarm Off in the Alarm dialog box and then click OK.
5. Click the Save and Close button on the Action bar to save your appointment.

VIEWING FREE TIME

When you invite others to a meeting, you can check their free time by selecting Click here to find free time for all invitees in the invitations section of your calendar entry. To create a calendar entry, invite others and see their free time:

1. From the Calendar view of your Mail database, click on the New Entry button on the Action bar.
2. Select Invitation as your calendar entry type.
3. Complete the Brief Description, Date and Time fields. If appropriate, complete the Detailed Description field.
4. Complete the Send Invitations to field. If you would like to invite others whose attendance you do not require, enter their names into the Optional Invitees field. You can type the names in the field or click on the down-arrow button to select the invitees from the Names dialog box

5. Choose Click here to find free time for all invitees to see their free time. The Free Time dialog box appears as shown in Figure 19.3. This box displays a white bar behind the name of each person whose free time is available for viewing (gray if it is not). Blue bars indicate busy times for each person, and a red or green bar represents the appointment you are creating. If your appointment bar is green, the time is OK for everyone, and that information is displayed on the left of the Free Time dialog box. If there is a conflict in schedules, the dialog box will display "Scheduled time is not OK for everyone," and the appointment bar will be red.

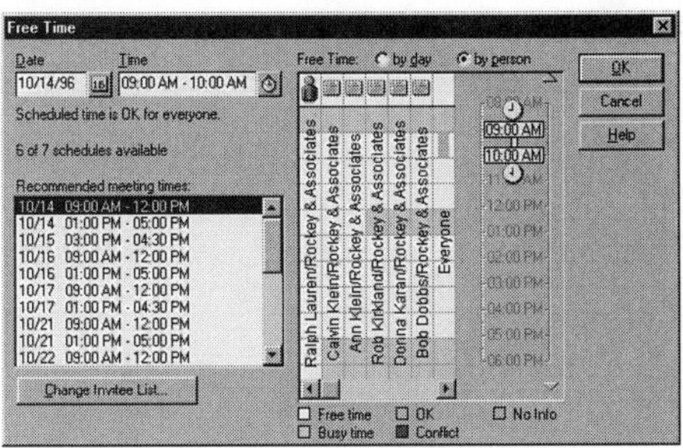

FIGURE 19.3 The Free Time dialog box.

6. If your scheduled time is not OK, you can change the Date and Time fields in the Free Time dialog box. You can also change the list of invitees by clicking on the Change Invitee List button of the dialog box.

7. When you are satisfied with your appointment, click on OK to close the dialog box.

8. Click the Save and Close button on the Action bar to save this calendar entry. Notes will send invitations to those listed in your Required and Optional Invitee lists.

This meeting will now appear in your calendar.

RESPONDING TO INVITATIONS

Invitations that you receive from others will appear in the Inbox view of your mail as well as the Meetings view. Meetings will only appear in your calendar if you created them yourself, save someone else the rights to create them, or accepted an invitation. Figure 19.4 shows an invitation from Ann Klein in the Inbox view of Mail.

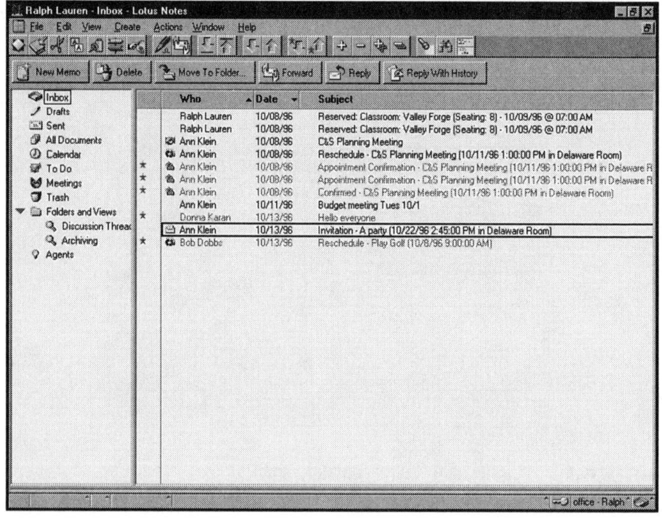

FIGURE 19.4 An Invitation displays in the Inbox view of Mail.

To respond to an invitation:

1. Open the invitation by double-clicking on it in your Meetings or Inbox view of Mail.

2. Select your response by using the buttons on the Action bar. (See Figure 19.6.) Those choices are:

   Accept mails an acceptance notice to the person who initiated the invitation and adds the meeting to your calendar.

Decline sends a regrets notification to the person who initiated the invitation.

Other gives you the option to Decline with comments, delegate this meeting to someone else (who will be automatically notified), or propose an alternate time or location.

FIGURE 19.6 Responding to an Invitation.

3. Choose the appropriate selection and click on OK to save and close the document.

In this lesson, you learned how to create calendar entries, invite others, and see the free time of others. You also learned how to respond to an invitation. In the next lesson, you will learn how to make e-mail look professional with formatting.

Lesson 20 Formatting Paragraphs

In this lesson, you learn how to format paragraphs in your e-mail messages.

Aligning and Indenting Paragraphs

Since Lotus Notes Mail is such a powerful word processor, many people write interoffice memos, proposals, and the like directly in the Lotus Notes Mail program. For those who travel with a laptop, Lotus Notes offers the possibility of not having to install a word processor, saving on disk space. In addition to formatting text as you learned in Lesson 7, Lotus Notes provides many tools for paragraph formatting. A paragraph, as defined in word processing, is any text that ends with a hard return (Enter).

You can change the alignment of a paragraph to make it flush left, flush right, centered, or justified.

1. Create a new mail message. In the body field, type several paragraphs.
2. Select the paragraphs you want to align.
3. Choose Text, Text Properties. The Text Properties box appears (see Figure 18.1).
4. Click the Alignment tab.
5. Click one of the alignment icons: Left, Center, Right, Full, No Wrap:

   Left Aligns text flush to the left margin but ragged on the right margin.

Center Centers text between the left and right margins.

Right Aligns text flush to the right margin but ragged on the left margin.

Full Aligns text flush with the left and right margins.

No Wrap Turns off word wrapping and displays text on one line.

6. Click the Close button (X). Your selected paragraphs are realigned.

Shortcuts You can also align paragraphs with the Text Align Paragraph Left, Text Align Paragraph Center, and Text Align Paragraph Right SmartIcons. Or you can choose Text, Align Paragraph and then select Left, Center, Right, Full, or No Wrap.

Lotus Notes gives you a number of ways to indent paragraphs. Indenting moves the beginning of the first line of the paragraph to the right by a specified amount. Outdenting moves the beginning of the first line of the paragraph to the left by a specified amount (also referred to as a hanging paragraph).

Setting indents using the Text Properties box:

1. Select the paragraph or paragraphs you want to indent.
2. Choose Text, Text Properties.
3. In the Text Properties box (see Figure 18.1), click the Alignment tab.

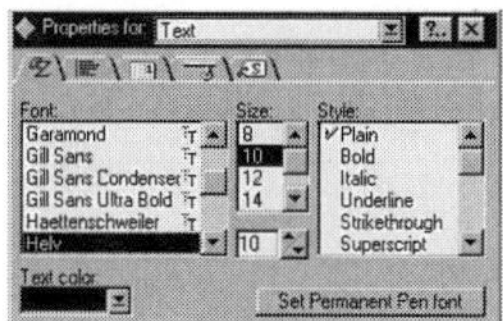

FIGURE 18.1 The Text Properties box.

4. Click a First line icon: Normal, Indent, or Outdent.

   Normal Keeps the margins at the default settings.

   Indent Starts the first line of the paragraph to the right of the left margin setting. You determine the spacing.

   Outdent Starts the first line of the paragraph at the margin setting, the rest of the paragraph is indented to the right. You determine the spacing.

5. When you select indented or outdented paragraphs, a new field appears on the Properties box. Enter the amount of space you want for your Indent or Outdent (.25" is the default).
6. The new formatting is applied. Click the Close (X) button if you want to close the Properties box.

You can also use the Ruler above the open message to set indents:

1. Select the paragraph or paragraphs to indent.
2. Choose View, Ruler. The Ruler appears above the open message (see Figure 18.2).

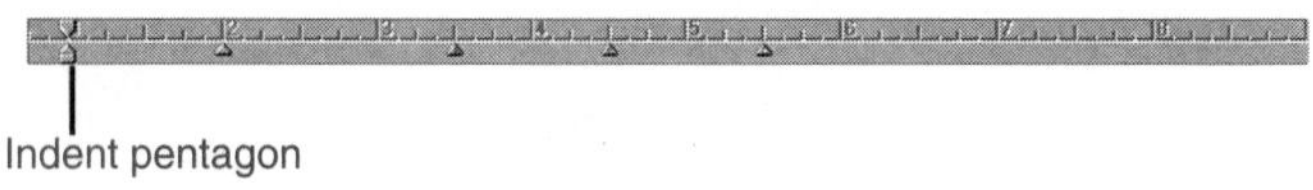

FIGURE 18.2 Ruler with indent pentagons.

3. Drag the upper pentagon pointer to where you want the first line of the paragraph(s) to start, drag the lower pentagon pointer to where you want the remaining lines of the selected paragraph(s) to start or drag the rectangle that sits beneath the pentagons to adjust all lines at once. If you drag the top or the bottom pentagon and meant to take both, simply double-click the one you moved. This will force the pentagons together again.

BULLETS AND NUMBERS

You can create bulleted or numbered lists to emphasize important information in your message. Use bullets for listing information when the order of the listing is not important. Use numbered lists when a logical sequence is critical to understanding the information, such as listing steps to complete a task.

You can convert text in existing paragraphs to a bulleted or numbered list simply by selecting the paragraphs and then clicking the Bullet or Number SmartIcon on the toolbar. Each paragraph becomes a separate bullet or number in the listing. Or you can first click the Bullet or Number SmartIcon; then begin typing the text. Each time you press Enter, a new bullet or the next number in sequence appears.

> TIP Automatic Renumbering If you decide you don't need one of the items in your numbered list, simply delete it, and Notes will automatically renumber the list if necessary.

LINE AND PARAGRAPH SPACING

You can set the spacing between lines in a paragraph, as well as the amount of space before and after paragraphs.

1. Select the paragraph(s) you want to change.
2. Choose Text, Text Properties.
3. In the Text Properties box, click the Alignment tab.
4. To set the spacing between lines within a paragraph, select Single, Double, 1 1/2 from the Interline list box.

5. To set the amount of space you want between paragraphs, select Single, Double, or 1½ from either the Above or Below list box

6. The new formatting is applied. Click the Close button (X) if you want to close the Properties box.

SETTING TABS

Tabs are set every ½ inch in Lotus Notes, but sometimes you need to set your own tabs. You can set tabs from the Text Properties box or from the Ruler.

From the Text Properties box:

1. Select the paragraph(s) for which you want to set tabs.

2. Choose Text, Text Properties, and then click the Page tab (see Figure 18.3).

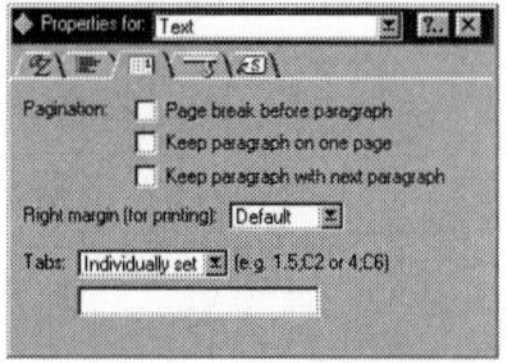

FIGURE 18.3 The Text Properties box with the Page tab selected.

3. In the Tabs drop-down list box, choose one of the following:

    - Individually set and enter the tab stops you want (if you enter more than one, separate them with semicolons).

    - Evenly spaced and enter the interval between tab stops. Always enter the numbers followed by the inch mark (").

4. (Optional) If you want to enter left, right, center, or decimal tabs, type an **L, R, C,** or **D** before the number (such as L1").

To set tabs using the Ruler:

1. Select the paragraph(s) to which you want to add tabs.
2. If you don't see the Ruler, choose View, Ruler.
3. On the Ruler (see Figure 18.4), click where you want a left tab, right-click where you want a right tab, press Shift and click where you want a decimal tab, and press Shift and right-click where you want a centered tab.

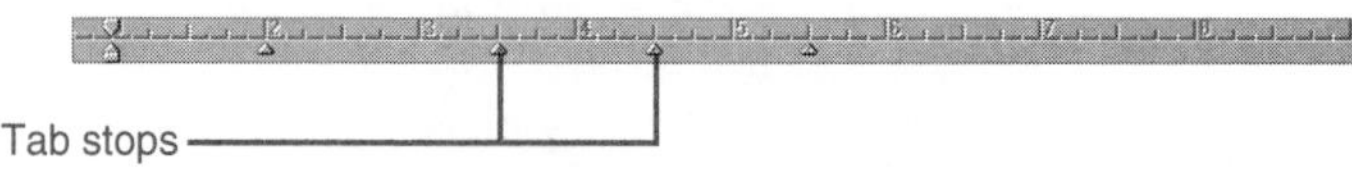

FIGURE 18.4 Ruler with tab stops.

To remove a tab from the Ruler, click it. To change the type of the tab, right-click the tab and select a tab type.

KEEPING PARAGRAPHS ON ONE PAGE OR TOGETHER

You may want to keep a paragraph from breaking in the middle when you have an automatic page break. You can enter a manual page break to control where your page breaks by choosing Create, Page Break where you want the new page to start. Alternatively, you can format the paragraph(s) to keep the lines all on one page. You may also want to be sure that two paragraphs are kept together and not split by the page break, which is especially important if one paragraph is a headline.

1. Click in the paragraph you want to keep on one page, or click in the first of two consecutive paragraphs you want to keep on that page.
2. Choose Text, Text Properties.
3. In the Text Properties box, click the Page tab (see Figure 18.5).

4. Under Pagination, select Keep paragraph on one page or Keep paragraph with next paragraph.

5. Click the Close (X) button if you want to close the Properties box.

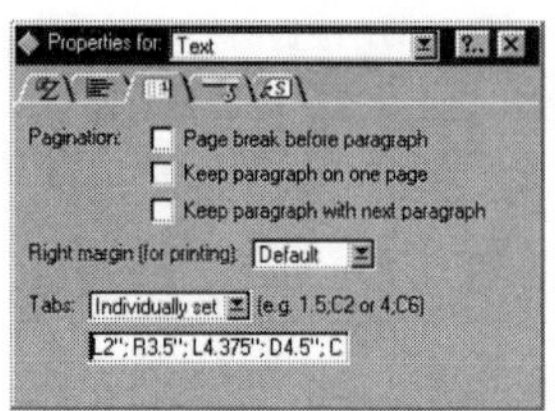

FIGURE 18.5 Text Properties box with Page tab selected.

To see the page breaks, choose View, Show, and Page Breaks. Page breaks appear as solid lines across the screen.

USING NAMED STYLES

If you use the same set of formatting commands frequently, it's time for you to try named styles. Named styles keep a group of formatting commands together, so you can apply them as a group:

1. Format a paragraph with the properties you want to save as a named style.

2. Click the paragraph.

3. Choose Text, Text Properties.

4. In the Text Properties box, click the Named Styles tab.

5. Click Create Style and enter a name for the paragraph style in the Style name text box (see Figure 18.6).

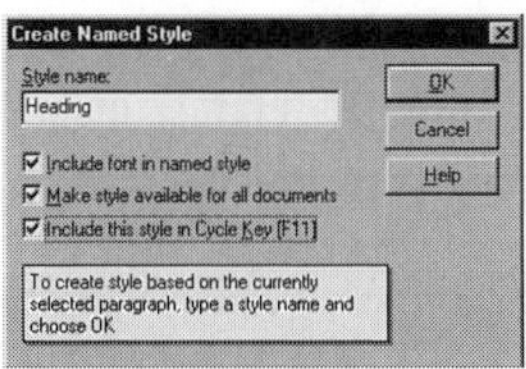

FIGURE 18.6 The Create Named Style dialog box.

6. Check any of the following options:
   - Check Include font in named style if you want to save the font as part of the named style.
   - Check Make style available for all documents if you want to use the named style outside of this one document.
   - Check Include this style in Cycle Key [F11] so it becomes one of the styles available when you press F11 to cycle through the named styles.
7. Click OK.

Once you create the named style, you can apply it to other paragraphs:

1. Select the paragraph(s) to which you want to apply the named style.
2. Choose Text, Named Styles, and select a style from the menu. Or click the Named Styles indicator on the status bar and select a style from the pop-up list.

If you need to change a named style, first format a paragraph with the new properties you want for the named style. Choose Text, Text Properties, and then click the Named Styles tab. Click Redefine Style and select the named style whose properties you want to replace with those of the selected paragraph. Then click OK.

To delete a named style, choose Text, Text Properties, and click the Named Styles tab. Click the Delete Styles button. Choose the name of the style you want to delete, and then click OK.

In this lesson, you learned about formatting paragraphs. In the next lesson, you learn some advanced formatting.

LESSON 21

ADVANCED FORMATTING

In this lesson, you learn about adding sections and tables to your Mail messages. You'll also learn how to format and change layout features of tables.

CREATING SECTIONS

Sections are helpful in making large documents more manageable. You can gather all the information on one topic into a section. Sections collapse into one-line paragraphs or expand to display all the text in the section, so a reader doesn't have to read sections that aren't of any interest. Figure 21.1 shows a document with collapsed sections.

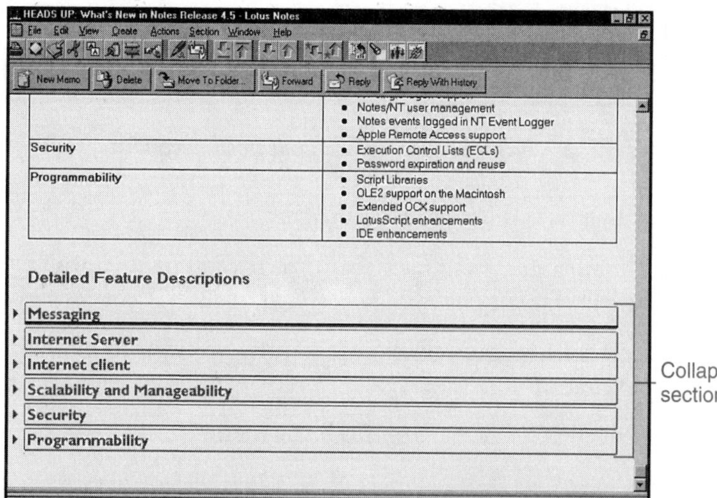

FIGURE 21.1 A document with collapsed sections.

When you gather text into a section, a small triangle appears to the left of the section head. To expand a section, click this triangle. Clicking again on the triangle collapses the section. To expand all the sections in a document, choose View, Expand All Sections from the menu. To collapse all sections, choose View, Collapse All Sections from the menu. Figure 21.2 shows a document with an expanded section.

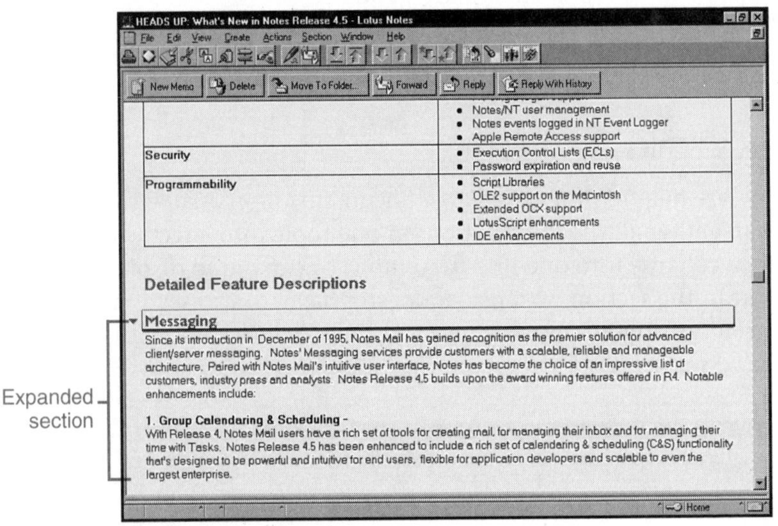

FIGURE 21.2 A document with an expanded section.

To create a section in your message:

1. Create a new mail message. Type several paragraphs in the body field.
2. Select the paragraph or paragraphs you want to make into a section.
3. Choose Create, Section from the menu.

The first paragraph of the section becomes the section title. If you want to change it, follow these steps:

1. Click the section title.
2. Choose Section, Section Properties from the menu (see Figure 21.3).

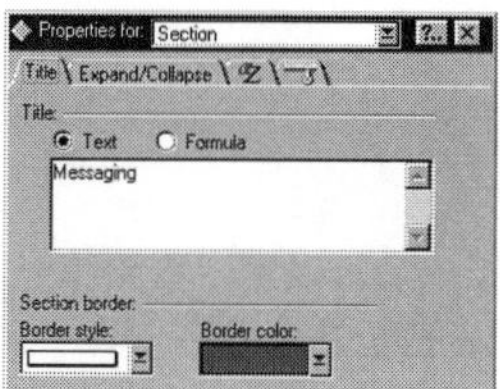

FIGURE 21.3 The Section Properties box with the Title tab chosen.

3. Click the Title tab.
4. Select Text, and then replace the text in the Title box with the section title you want. Don't use carriage returns, hotspots, or buttons in section titles.
5. Under Section Border, choose a Border style from the list box and a Border color from the list box.
6. If you want to hide the title of the section when it expands, click the Expand/Collapse tab, and check Hide title when expanded (see Figure 21.4).

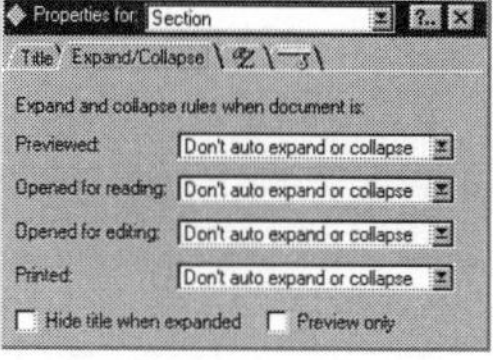

FIGURE 21.4 The Section Properties box with the Expand/Collapse tab chosen.

If you want to format the section title, select it and choose Text, Text Properties. Click the Font tab; then select the font, size, style, and color you want for the section title.

To move a section from one part of a document to another, select the section and choose Edit, Cut. Position your cursor where you want the section to appear. Choose Edit, Paste.

When you want to remove a section, but still want to keep all the text in the section, select the section and choose Section, Remove Section. However, if you want to remove the section and all its text, choose Edit, Clear.

INSERTING TABLES

Tables offer an excellent way to organize data, and you can easily add tables to your mail messages. Figure 21.5 shows a mail message with a table inserted.

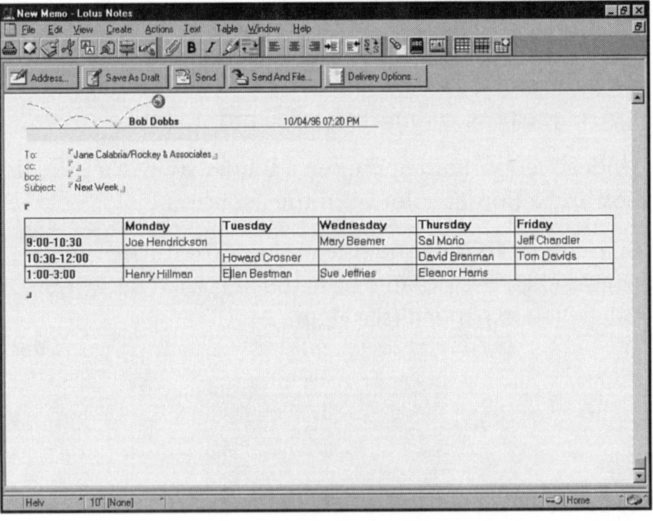

FIGURE 21.5 A mail message with table inserted.

To insert a table in your mail message:

1. Create a new memo.
2. Position your cursor in the body field where you want the table to appear.

3. Choose Create, Table or click the Create Table SmartIcon. The Create Table dialog box appears (see Figure 21.6).

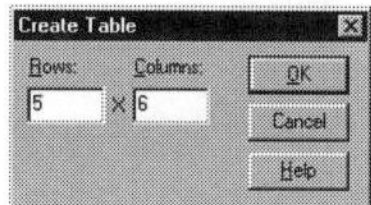

FIGURE 21.6 The Create Table dialog box.

4. Enter the number of Rows and Columns you want in your table.
5. Click OK.

INSERTING, DELETING, COPYING, AND MOVING COLUMNS AND ROWS

If you didn't specify the correct number of columns or rows when you created the table, you can insert or delete columns or rows.

To insert one column or row:

1. Click in the column or row where you want to insert a new one. New columns appear to the left of the column your cursor is in; new rows appear above the row your cursor is in.
2. Choose Table, Insert Column or Table, Insert Row from the menu.

To add a row at the bottom of the table or a column at the right of the table, choose Table, Append Row or Table, Append Column from the menu.

To add more than one column or row, position your cursor and choose Table, Insert Special. Specify the number of columns or rows you want to add and choose Column(s) or Row(s). Click Insert (see Figure 21.7).

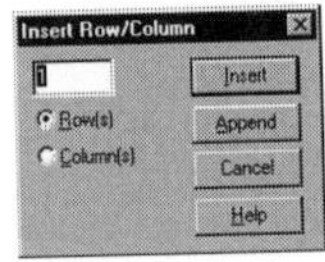

FIGURE 21.7 The Insert Row/Column dialog box.

To delete a column or row, click in the row or column you want to remove. Choose Table, Delete Selected Column(s) or Table, Delete Selected Row(s). Click Yes to confirm the deletion. *Remember*: deleting a column or row also deletes all the text in that column or row.

To delete several columns or rows, place your cursor in the first column or row of the ones you want to delete. Choose Table, Delete Special. Specify the number of columns or rows you want to delete, select Column(s) or Row(s), and click Delete. Choose Yes to confirm the deletion.

Delete the Text, Not the Table! You don't have to delete columns or rows to delete the text. If you want to leave your columns and rows intact, select the text and choose Edit, Clear or press Delete.

You can use Edit, Copy to copy rows or columns of data in a table. Edit, Cut will remove selected columns or rows and store them in the Clipboard. You can then use Edit, Paste to put them in a new position (where you have your cursor).

FORMATTING TABLES

You can also control how your table looks. You can put borders around the outside of the table or around each cell. You can set the width of the columns and the space between columns and rows; and you can determine the overall width of the table.

To set borders on the table:

1. Select the cells of the table to which you want to add borders.
2. Choose Table, Table Properties from the menu. Figure 21.8 shows the Table Properties box.

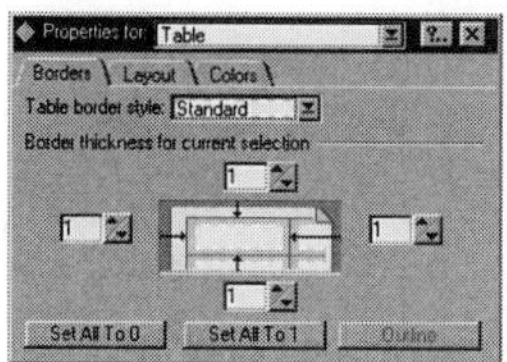

FIGURE 21.8 The Table Properties box with the Cell Borders tab selected.

3. Click the Borders tab. You can choose how you want your borders to look:

   - To set the type of lines you want to use as borders for your cells, choose Standard, Extruded, or Embossed from the Table border style list box.
   - Click Outline to set the borders for *only* the outside lines of the current selection.
   - To set the borders on all sides to single, click the Set All to Single button.
   - To not have any borders, click the Set All to None button.
   - To set the sides individually, specify the number of lines for each side (0 equals none, 1 equals single, 2 equals double, and so on).

To set the overall width of the table, so the column widths will adjust to fit the table in the window:

1. Click anywhere in the table.
2. Choose Table, Table Properties from the menu. The Table Properties box appears.
3. Click the Layout tab.
4. Select Fit table width to window to automatically size the table to fit the window.

Here are a few more changes you can make to the layout of your table:

1. Click anywhere in the table.
2. Choose Table, Table Properties from the menu.
3. Click the Layout tab (see Figure 21.9).

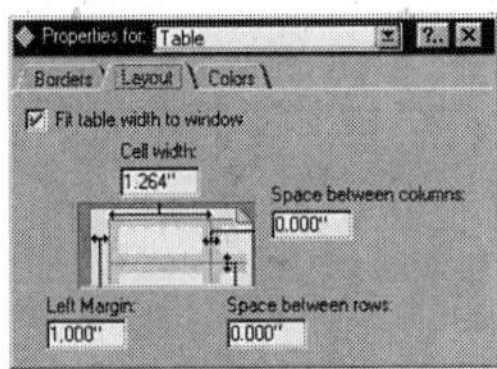

FIGURE 21.9 The Table Properties box with the Layout tab selected.

4. Set any of the following layout features:

   - To set the left margin of the table, enter a new value in the Left Margin box.
   - To set the spacing between the columns and rows, enter a new value in Space between columns and/or Space between rows.
   - To change the column width, remove the check mark from Fit table width to window and enter the new width in the Cell width box.

You can also set the column width using the Ruler:

1. Click in the column you want to modify.
2. If you don't see the Ruler, choose View, Ruler from the menu.
3. The column has two thin bar pointers on the Ruler. Drag the first one to show where the column starts; drag the second one to where the column ends.

You can also add color to the cells in your table or to the entire table:

1. Select the cell or cells you want to color.
2. Choose Table, Table Properties from the menu.
3. Click the Colors tab.
4. Select the color you want to use from the Background color drop-down list.
5. If you want the same background for all the cells in the table, click Apply to Entire Table.
6. If you want the cell background to be transparent, click Make Transparent.

In this lesson, you learned how to create sections in your mail messages. You also learned how to add and format tables. In the next section, you learn about security.

Understanding Security

In this lesson, you learn about the Access Control List and how it affects you. You also learn how encryption and signatures protect your documents.

Passwords

Your first line of defense in keeping your system and mail secure from unauthorized people is your password. When you access the Lotus Notes server the first time you start Notes, you see a prompt asking you to enter your password. You won't see what you are typing, but then neither can anyone else.

Your password can be any combination of keyboard characters, as long as the first character is a letter of the alphabet. Make your password at least eight characters long, and remember that passwords are case-sensitive. The password "INFONUT" is different than the password "infonut."

You can change your password at any time:

1. Choose File, Tools, User ID from the menu (see Figure 22.1).
2. Enter your current password if you are asked and then click OK.
3. Click the Set Password button.
4. Enter your new password.
5. Click OK.

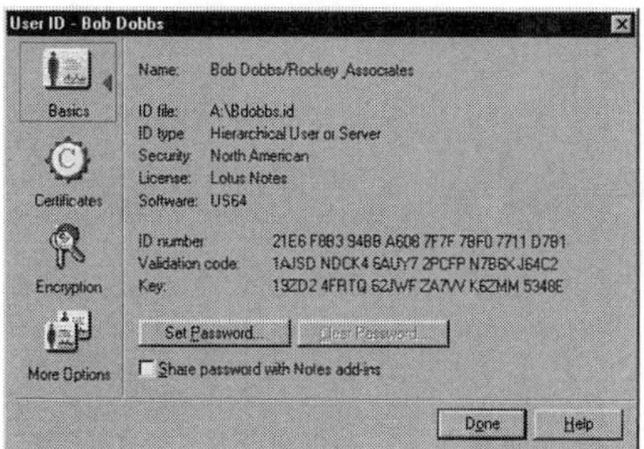

FIGURE 22.1 The User ID dialog box.

6. Type the password again, exactly as you did the first time, to confirm it.
7. Click OK.
8. Click Done.

The user ID is a file created when the Notes administrator first registers you as a user. When you start up Lotus Notes on your computer for the first time, that file transfers to your computer and by default is placed in the \Notes\Data directory or folder. You want to be careful to protect that file, since someone else could use it to pretend to be you on the Lotus Notes network. If your computer operating system is password protected, that may be enough. But if your computer is accessible to several people, you might want to move it out of your computer onto a floppy disk for safekeeping. If you ever suspect it is lost (along with your stolen laptop), you should report it to the Notes administrator.

THE ACCESS CONTROL LIST

Lotus Notes has several features designed to limit access to documents, views, databases, or servers. For example, only authorized personnel are permitted to delete databases from the server, design applications, open certain documents, or read designated fields. The Notes administrator or the Application Designer controls most of this. What you are authorized to do depends on your status in the Access Control List.

To find your level of access for a particular database, click the database icon to select it; then click the Access Key button on the status bar. A dialog box appears that tells you what your access is (see Figure 22.2). To see your access, highlight your name in the list box.

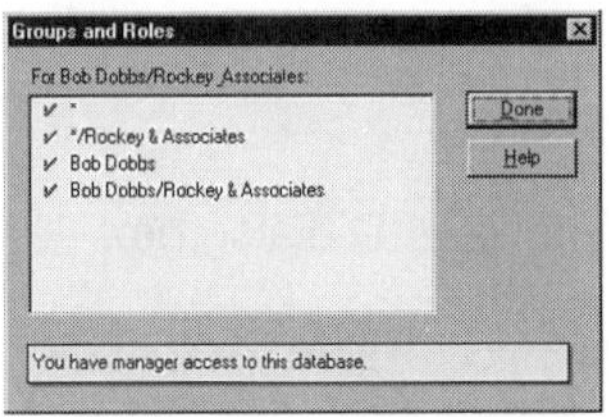

FIGURE 22.2 The Groups and Roles dialog box.

You may be granted any one of seven levels of access to a database:

- **No Access** Denies you access to the database. You can't read any of the documents in the database and you can't create new documents. In fact, you cannot add the database icon to your workspace if you have do not have access.
- **Depositor** You can create documents but can't read any of the documents in the database—including the ones you create yourself. You might be granted this access level to cast a ballot in a voting database, for example.
- **Reader** You can read the documents in the database, but you can't create or edit documents. You might have this level of access to a company policy database, so you can read policies but can't create or change them.
- **Author** As an author, you can create documents and edit your own documents. However, you can't edit documents created by others even though you can read them.
- **Editor** You can do everything an author does, plus you can edit documents submitted by others. A manager who

approves the expense reports submitted by others needs editor access to those documents.

- **Designer** A designer can do everything an editor does, but can also create or change any design elements of the database. In order to create a new call report database in Notes, for instance, you would have to be a designer.
- **Manager** Can access everything a designer can. A manager can also assign and modify the access control list (ACL), modify replication settings, and delete a database from the server.

You will probably have at least reader access to the Public Address Book, while you have manager access to your personal address book. It's wise to limit the number of people who can modify the Public Address Book, so everyone in the company is properly listed and no one is accidentally deleted. However, you can do whatever you like to your own Personal Address Book because you aren't sharing it with anyone.

ENCRYPTION

When you want to keep your mail private, encrypt it. Encrypting scrambles your message so it can only be read by the person receiving it.

Each Lotus Notes user has a unique *private* and *public* key that Notes stores as part of the ID file. The public key is also stored in the person document for each user in the Public Address Book. When someone sends you a mail message and chooses to encrypt it, Notes uses your public key from the Public Address Book to encrypt the message. Now, no one but you can read it. At the delivery end, Notes uses your private key from your ID file to decrypt the message so you can read it.

To encrypt a mail message:

1. Create the memo.

2. Click the Delivery Options button on the Action bar. The Delivery Options dialog box appears (see Figure 22.3).

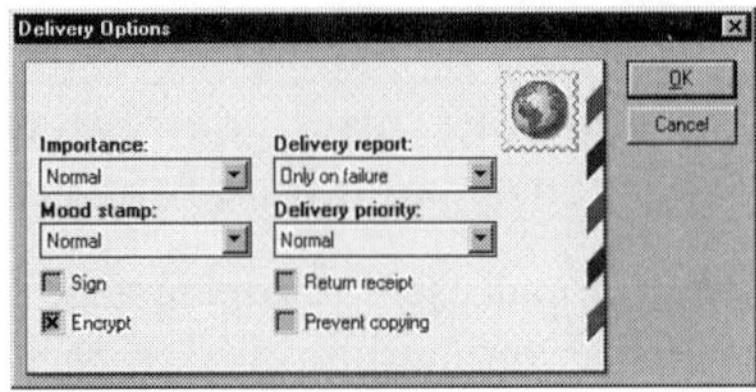

FIGURE 22.3 The Delivery Options dialog box.

3. Check Encrypt.
4. Click OK.

To encrypt all the mail messages you send:

1. Choose File, Tools, User Preferences.
2. In the User Preferences dialog box (see Figure 22.4), click the Mail icon.
3. Check Encrypt sent mail.
4. Click OK.

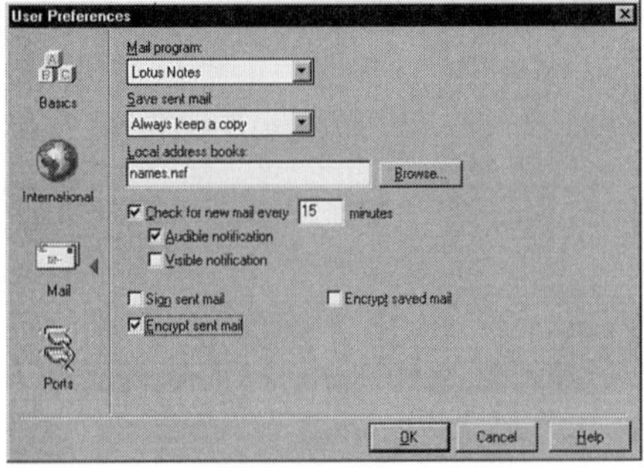

FIGURE 22.4 User Preferences with Mail selected.

If you want to encrypt all the mail that comes to you:

1. From the workspace, double-click the icon for your Public Address Book to open it.
2. Double-click the People folder to open it.
3. Open the document that shows your name (your person document).
4. Choose Actions, Edit Person.
5. In Encrypt Incoming Mail, enter Yes.
6. Save and close the document.
7. Close the Public Address Book.

Can't Save Your Person Document? If you can't save the document or you can't make the change, you'll have to ask your Notes administrator to do it for you. You may not have sufficient access to the Public Address Book to make modifications, not even to your own person document.

SIGNATURES

When you want the recipient of your mail message to know that it is coming from you, add a digital signature to your message to let your recipient know that no one has tampered with your message. Even if someone obtains a copy of your Notes user ID file, that person cannot forge your signature with it.

To sign an individual message:

1. Create a memo.
2. Click the Delivery Options button on the Action bar.
3. The Delivery Options dialog box appears (see Figure 22.3).

4. Check Sign.
5. Click OK.

If you want to add a signature to all your messages:

1. Choose File, Tools, User Preferences.
2. Click the Mail icon (see Figure 22.4).
3. Check Sign sent mail.
4. Click OK.

In this lesson, you learned about Lotus Notes security and how to secure your own mail by using encryption and signatures. In the next lesson, you learn about setting up Notes for use outside the office.

Setting Up for Mobile Use

In this lesson, you learn how to prepare to use Lotus Notes Mail remotely. You learn how to tell Lotus Notes what kind of modem you use and your location, and how to dial into the Lotus Notes server.

What You Need to Go Remote

Remote users are those who work with Lotus Notes on a laptop or desktop, and who are not constantly connected to the Lotus Notes server.

To work remotely, from home, a hotel room, or a location outside of the office in which you are not connected to your local area network, you need:

- A computer with Lotus Notes 4.5 or Notes Mail installed.
- A modem connected to your PC.
- A phone line for your modem.

You also need the following information from your Lotus Notes administrator:

- The name of your Lotus Notes server.
- The phone number of the Lotus Notes server.
- A copy of your certified Notes User ID (if you don't already have it).

WORKING WITH CONNECTION DOCUMENTS

To use Lotus Notes Mail remotely, you must provide information about your server: the name of your server, the phone number to dial for your server, and the *type* of connection you are making (such as dial-in). You provide this information in a *Server Connection document.*

Many companies have support people who can configure the laptop for you. But in some cases, you may have Lotus Notes Mail installed on your PC at home, or you might be a field person located far from the home office. In that situation, you need to perform the steps described in this lesson. Before you begin, ask your Lotus Notes administrator for the name of your Lotus Notes Mail server and the phone number to dial into the server.

To create a Server Connection document:

1. From your workspace, double-click your Personal Address Book.
2. Select the Server, Connections view.
3. Click the Add Connection button on the Action bar.
4. The Server Connection document appears as seen in Figure 23.1. Select the Connection Type as Dialup Modem.
5. Type the name of your Mail database server in the Server name field.
6. Fill in the Area code and Phone number fields.

   If your server has more than one phone number, fill in the additional phone numbers by pressing the Enter key between phone numbers. If you supply more than one phone number, and the first number is busy, Lotus Notes will automatically try dialing the second number, then the third number, and so on, until the server answers the telephone.

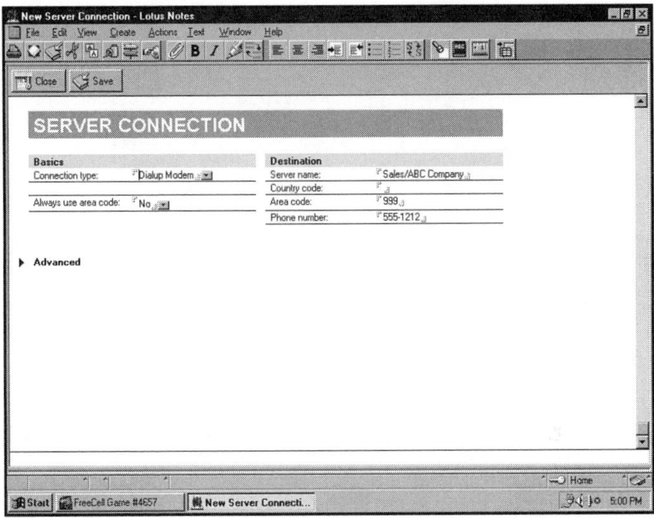

FIGURE 23.1 The Server Connection document.

7. Click the Save button on the Action bar to save this Server Connection document and close this window.

If you are going to call into more than one server, you need a Server Connection document for each. The exception is the use of a *Passthru* server. You'll learn more about the Passthru server in the Location Documents section of this lesson.

CONFIGURING PORTS AND MODEMS

Now that you have established what server you're connecting to, you need to specify the type of modem you're using and which port it uses.

1. Choose File, Tools, User Preferences from the menu.
2. In the User Preferences dialog box, click the Ports icon (see Figure 23.2).

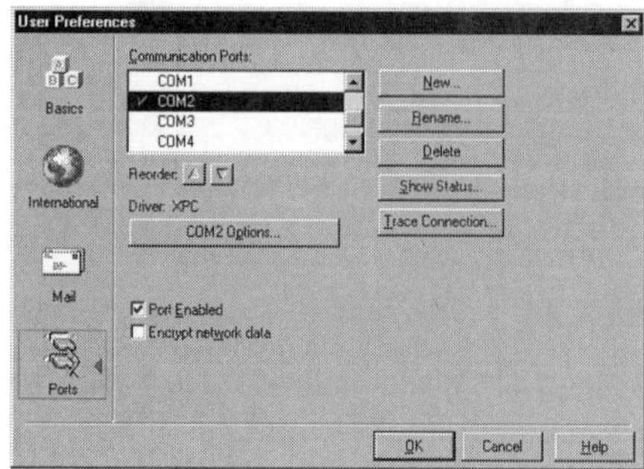

FIGURE 23.2 The User Preferences dialog box.

3. Pick the port your modem uses, such as COM1 or COM2.
4. Check Port Enabled.
5. Click the Options button (the name of the port is on the button). The Additional Setup dialog box appears as shown in Figure 23.3.

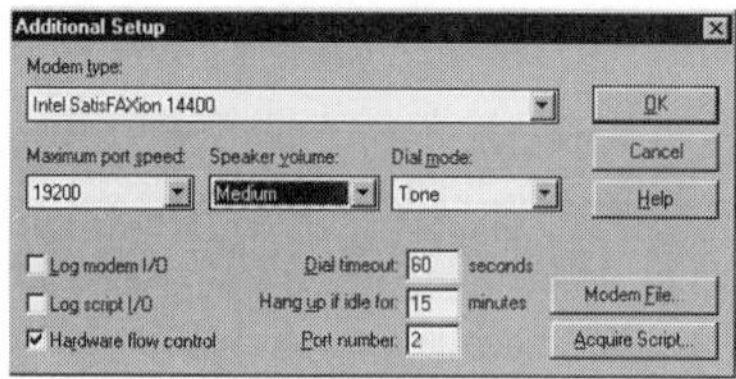

FIGURE 23.3 Additional Setup dialog box.

6. Specify the Modem type you have (use the Autoconfigure or generic all-speed modem type if you don't know) and enter any settings you need for your modem.
7. Click OK to exit the dialog box.
8. Click OK to exit User Preferences.

CREATING LOCATION DOCUMENTS

The Location document contains such information as how you connect to the network, what port you use, where your Mail file is, telephone numbers for dialing in, and a replication schedule.

Five location documents automatically appear during the installation process: Home (Modem), Office (Network), Travel (Modem), Island (Disconnected), and Internet. You'll find them in your Personal Address Book in the Locations view. You can customize them to suit your needs or create your own Location documents.

Typically, the Office location is the one you use when you are in the office, connected to the LAN via a network port. Home is set up for a remote connection, via modem, as is Travel. In the Travel Location document, however, you may want to specify your area code so Notes will dial 1 and the area code of your home server. The Home and Travel documents assume you are using a local replica of your Mail database.

To customize the Home Location document you'll need to provide information in five of the eight sections. To complete the Location document:

1. If the location indicated on the status bar is not "Home," then click the location indicated on the status bar and choose Home as your location. "Home" is now your "current" location.
2. Click Home on the status bar and choose Edit current. You'll see the Location document for Home location (see Figure 23.4).
3. In the Basics section, choose one of four options in Location type:
    - Local Area Network If you need to connect to a LAN or WAN.
    - Dialup Modem If you plan to communicate via a modem.

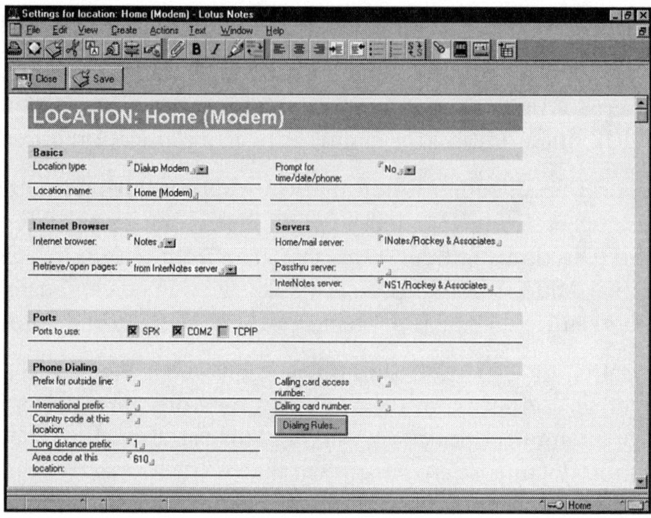

FIGURE 23.4 A Location document.

- Both Dialup and Local Area Network If you have both a network connection and want to use the modem from the same location.
- No Connection If you want to use Notes but will not be connected to any Notes server.

4. In the Ports section, check the port you use for the location in the Ports to use field. The available ports are those you already enabled.
5. In the Servers section, enter the name of your home server in the Home/mail server field. Your home server is the server you connect to at work that stores your Mail database. Type its full name (for example, Sales/ABC Company is the name of the server Sales in the organization ABC Company).
6. If you use a Passthru server, specify the name of that server in the Passthru server field.

Passthru Server Some companies have many Lotus Notes servers. They may determine that one of those servers will act as the traffic controller for incoming calls; this is referred to as a *Passthru* server. Ask your Lotus Notes administrator if you're going to be dialing into a Passthru server. You need the Passthru server name and telephone number, as well as the server name that contains your Mail database.

7. In the Phone Dialing section (see Figure 23.5) complete the following:
    - Prefix for outside line Enter the number you dial to get an outside line (leave blank if there isn't one).
    - International prefix Enter the number to dial to make international calls (leave blank if you don't plan to call outside the country).
    - Country code at this location Enter the country code for your location (US is United States). Leave this blank if you are in the United States and calling within the United States.
    - Long distance prefix Notes enters a 1 here, but you may change it if you are outside the United States.
    - Area code at this location Enter the area code for the location.
    - Calling card access number To use a calling card, enter the number you need to dial before you dial the phone number. For an automatic delay in dialing, enter commas in the phone number. Each comma causes a two-second delay.
    - Calling card number Enter your calling card number.

- Dialing Rules   Click this button to use a different telephone number for a server at the location. Select the server, enter a different dialing prefix and phone number, and then click OK.

8. In the Mail section (see Figure 23.5) complete the following:

    - Mail file location   Choose Local to use a local replica of your Mail file or On server if you connect directly to the server.
    - Mail file   Enter the path and file name of your Mail file.

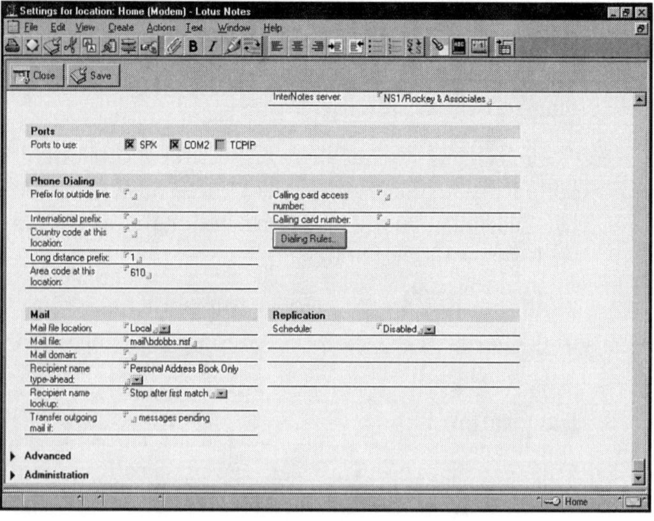

Figure 23.5 The Phone Dialing and Mail sections of the Location document.

The remaining fields on this form contain default information or don't apply to Mail options. Consult with your Notes administrator if you're using an InterNotes server. Click the Save button on the Action bar to save the file and the Close button to close the document.

Before you begin replicating (see Lessons 24 and 25) or before you send or receive mail, you must select the location with the correct communications settings.

1. Click the Location button on the status bar.
2. Select the location you want to use.

If you need to edit a location, click the Edit Location button on the Action bar in the Locations view of your Personal Address Book. Or click the Location button on the status bar and select Edit current. To delete a location document, click the Delete button on the Action bar in the Locations view of your Personal Address Book.

In this lesson, you learned how to set up Lotus Notes for mobile use. In the next lesson, you learn about creating a Mail replica.

LESSON

24 Creating a New Mail Replica

In this lesson, you learn about replication, how to create a new Mail replica, and how to copy from the Public Address Book.

Understanding Replication

Your home server in the office stores a number of databases. When you are in the office and connected to the network, you can open databases on the server directly from your workstation.

When you are not in the office, however, you can only access the server by using a modem. If you have a lot of work to do in a database, (such as reading and replying to mail) staying on the phone line can be costly. Also, working via modem is much slower than being on the network in the office.

Lotus Notes lets you read and reply to mail offline through *replication,* the process of "synchronizing" the same databases on different computers. It is actually a special type of copying process. Replication does not overwrite the entire database file. It only updates the documents you modified, and it does the same thing for everyone who replicates the database. Then as people call in and replicate a database, they get the most recent copy of the documents in the database on their own computers. The server receives their changes, and the server sends them any updates that have occurred since they last replicated. Eventually, the modifications get around to everyone using the database.

HOW REPLICATION WORKS

When you are ready to replicate a database, you place a telephone call from your computer (using your modem) to the server in your office. Once the two computers "shake hands" and recognize each other, your computer begins sending any updates you made to the database replicas. Then your computer receives any modifications made to the database since you last replicated.

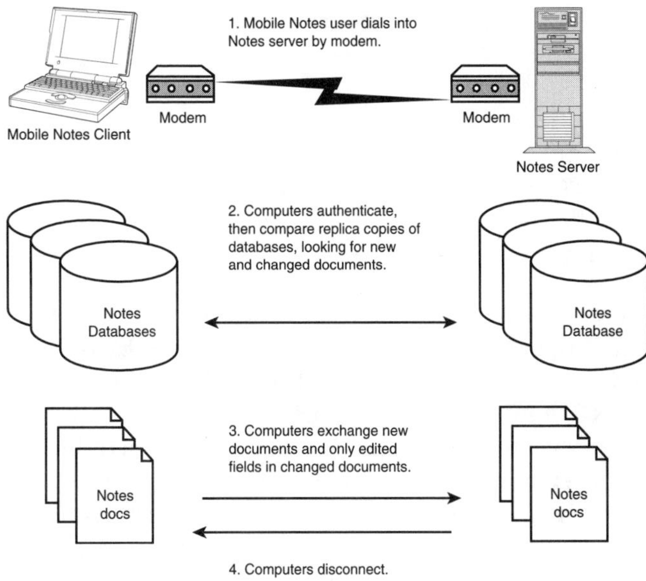

FIGURE 24.1 How replication works.

Each database has a unique *replica ID* that identifies it as a genuine replica, and not just a copy of the database (see Figure 24.2). If the database on your computer does not have the same ID as the one on the server, the server won't replicate the database.

Before replicating, the server also checks to see when the database on your computer was last modified. If that date is more recent than the date the database was last successfully replicated, then the database replicates. Lotus Notes maintains a replication history of each database you replicate (see Figure 24.3).

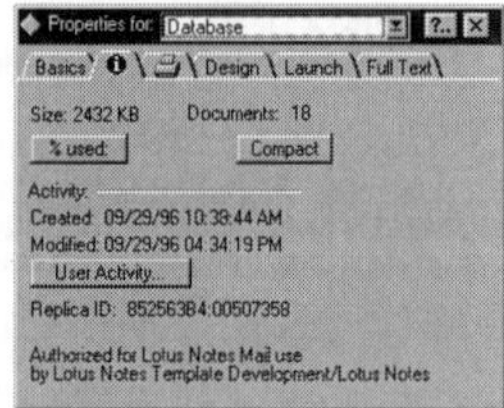

FIGURE 24.2 The replica ID.

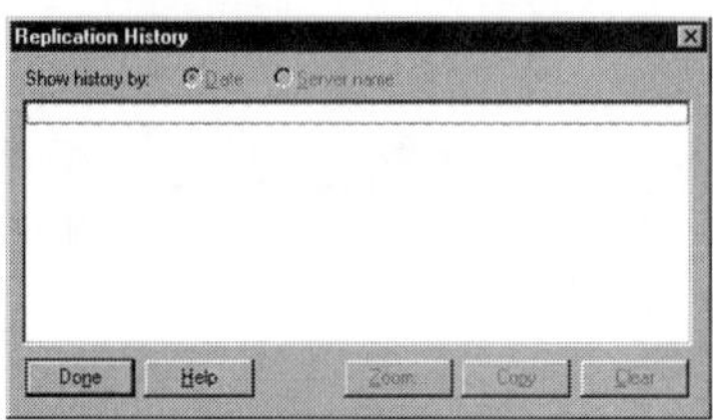

FIGURE 24.3 The replication history.

When the database replicates, it updates only those documents that have been changed since the last replication. Each document has its own unique Notes identification number assigned to it when it is first saved (see Figure 24.4). Part of that number is a document-level sequence number that increases each time you modify the document. If the number is higher for a particular document than the database on the server, then it gets replicated to the server.

When replication is complete, you'll hang up. You'll now have an updated copy of the database on your PC.

FIGURE 24.4 A unique Notes identification number.

CREATING A NEW MAIL REPLICA

Once you set up your computer for mobile use, as described in Lesson 23, the next step you should take is to create a new Mail replica. You need to call the server to do this. This step is only necessary if you don't see your Mail database on your workspace. You should also talk with your Notes administrator and confirm with him that you need a new Mail replica.

CALLING THE SERVER

To place a call from your computer to the server:

1. Choose File, Mobile, Call Server from the menu. The Call Server dialog box appears (see Figure 24.5).
2. Pick the name of the server you want to call (if you have more than one).
3. Click Auto Dial.

FIGURE 24.5 The Call Server dialog box.

If you call from a location that requires you to call an operator first before placing an outside call:

1. Choose File, Mobile, Call Server.
2. Click More Options. The expanded Call Server dialog box appears as shown in Figure 24.6.
3. Click Manual Dial.
4. When you see the Notes prompt, pick up the phone and call the operator.

5. Once the operator connects you to the outside line, dial the phone number of your server.
6. When the connection is made, hang up the phone and click OK.

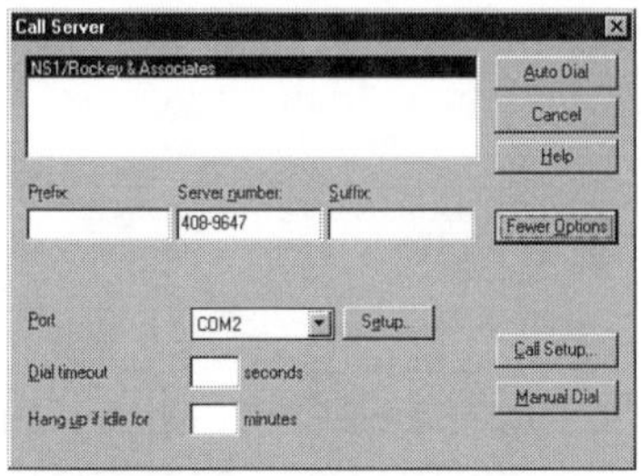

FIGURE 24.6 The expanded Call Server dialog box.

MAKING NEW REPLICAS

Making a new replica is a one-step process. When you finish this lesson, Lesson 25 will show you how to update this replica on an ongoing basis. It's very important to make a new replica of a database only once:

1. Choose File, Replication, New Replica; or click the New Replica SmartIcon.
2. The Choose Database dialog box appears (see Figure 24.7).

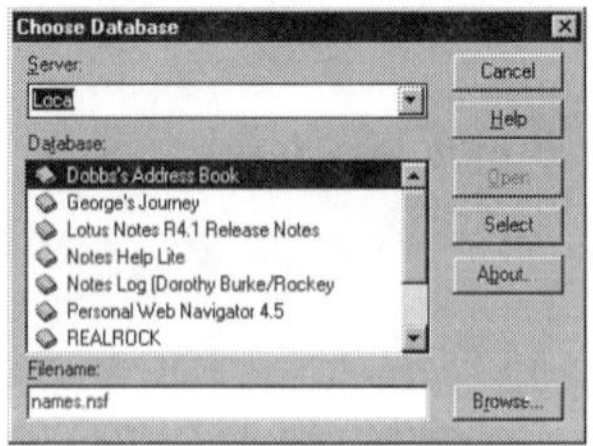

FIGURE 24.7 The Choose Database dialog box.

3. Under Server, choose your home server (if you are not currently connected, Lotus Notes will prompt you to call the server).
4. From the Database list, select the file you want to replicate. Mail files are usually located in the \Mail subdirectory or folder, and your Mail file has your name on it.
5. Click Select.
6. In the New Replica dialog box (see Figure 24.8), type the same title for your database as you saw in Figure 24.7. Notes does not automatically fill in the title field.

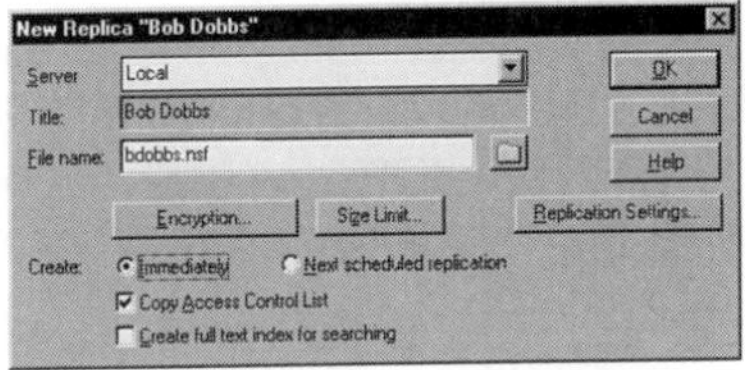

FIGURE 24.8 The New Replica dialog box.

7. Use the same file name for your database as indicated on the server copy.
8. Under Create, click Immediately.
9. Remove the check mark from Copy Access Control List.
10. Click OK.

After this, any time you want to replicate (update) your mail you'll use the Replicator page as shown in Lesson 25.

COPYING ADDRESSES TO THE PERSONAL ADDRESS BOOK

Now that you can create and send Mail messages from outside the office, make sure that you have the addresses you need in your Personal Address Book. You have two choices here: either copy information from the Public Address Book into your Personal Address Book as described here, or make a local copy of the Public Address Book as described under "Replicating the Public Address Book" that immediately follows.

1. While still online with your home server, choose File, Database, Open.
2. Under Server, select the name of your home server.
3. From the Database list, choose the name of your Public Address Book.
4. Click Open.
5. Open the People view.
6. Click in the left margin next to the names of the people documents you want to copy. A check mark will appear in front of each name to show it's selected.
7. Choose Edit, Copy, or click the Edit Copy SmartIcon.
8. Press ESC to return to your workspace.
9. Open your Personal Address Book by double-clicking its icon and open the People view.
10. Choose Edit, Paste or click the Edit Paste SmartIcon.

In this lesson, you learned about replication, making a new Mail replica and copying addresses from the Public Address Book to your Personal Address Book. In the next lesson, you learn how Mail works for mobile users.

LESSON 25

Using Mail Remotely

In this lesson, you learn about how Mail works for mobile users, how to use the Outgoing Mail database, how to set Mail send options, and how to receive and send mail.

Understanding Mail for Mobile Users

When you disconnect from the office network, either by working at a desktop computer outside the office (perhaps at home) or by using a laptop computer from a client site, a regional office, home, or hotel, you become a *mobile* user. You connect to the Notes network via a modem, instead of a LAN or WAN.

This makes a significant difference in the way you handle your mail. Although your Mail database is still on your Notes home server, connecting via modem and working online to create, send, receive, read, and organize your mail is time-consuming and possibly expensive if you're calling long distance.

Therefore, mobile users generally replicate their Mail databases to their laptops or desktops at home. You can work in your local replica, saving phone time for the replication process (see Lesson 24 for more about replication). You can access your data quickly, make and store all new documents and updates, and send everything to the server in one burst. You don't have to wait for a memo to be sent before you start the next one. In addition, once you initiate replication, you can continue working on your databases because replication works in the background.

Because you are working locally, addressing the mail is also a little different. When you enter the name of the recipient, Lotus Notes refers first to your Personal Address Book. If the addressee is not there, the assumption is that the recipient must be in the Public Address Book and will be found during replication. Therefore, you won't get a nondelivery report until after the mail has replicated. You might find it helpful to replicate the Public Address Book or at least copy the important addresses to your Personal Address Book to avoid this problem as discussed in Lesson 24.

USING THE OUTBOX

When you installed Lotus Notes on your remote computer or laptop, you specified that you would be using a remote connection. As part of the installation process, Notes then created a replica *stub* (or place holder) of your Mail database; all you had to do was replicate your Mail database documents to it, as you did in Lesson 24.

Because you are working with a local replica and not directly with the server, your mail isn't immediately delivered. Instead, when you choose to send a memo, Notes stores it temporarily in the Outgoing Mail database (to see the mail that is waiting to be sent, double-click on the Send outgoing mail icon on your workspace). Then when you choose to send the mail to the server or when you replicate the Mail database with the server, the outgoing mail is transferred and sent. The outgoing mailbox is emptied.

WHAT IS THE REPLICATOR PAGE?

When you work from a local replica of your Mail database, Lotus Notes creates an automatic Send outgoing mail entry on the Replicator page, as shown in Figure 25.1.

The Replicator page is the last page of your workspace, and it's the one workspace tab that you can't delete. The Replicator page provides a central location to handle all your replication needs. Using the features available on the Replicator page, you can set options to control replication of your mail and any other databases you may be using.

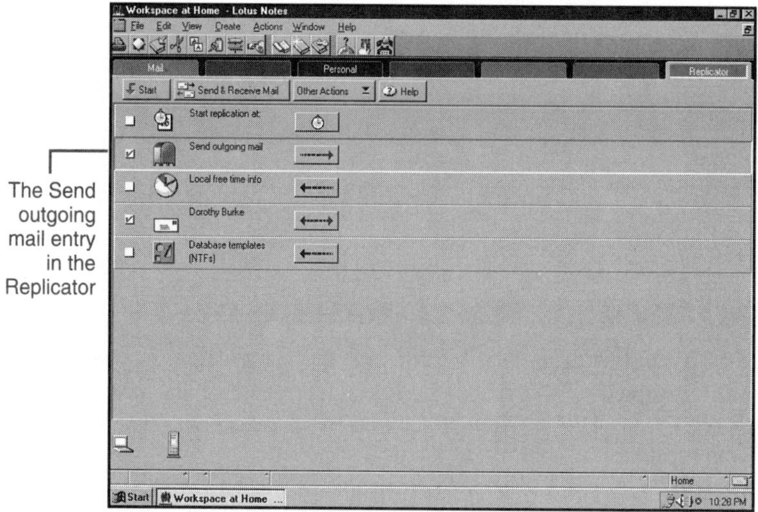

FIGURE 25.1 The Replicator page.

There are several rows, or *entries*, on the Replicator page:

Start Replication at Sets a schedule for replication; you can't delete or move this entry. Most people do not schedule their replications, since that would require that you turn on your PC and run Notes during the scheduled time. You'll usually use replication on demand, so you don't need to set this option.

Send outgoing mail Sends all pending messages from your mailbox.

Database templates Refreshes the designs of any template-based databases you have. You can't delete this entry. Don't worry about it; it doesn't affect mail.

Call and Hangup In addition to the automatic entry rows, you can create Call and Hangup entries for mobile locations.

For each local database replica you have, you also see a database entry on the Replicator page. You can replicate these databases at the same time you replicate your mail. Click the check box (a check mark appears) at the beginning of the database entry row to include it in the next replication when you click the Start button on the Action bar.

The status bar at the bottom of the page shows information about the current replication, letting you know when Lotus Notes is attempting to call a server, what database is being replicated, the progress of the replication, how many minutes are left, and when the replication is finished. After replication, the status bar displays statistics for individual entries.

Making Call and Hangup Entries

If you are a mobile user, you'll want to create call entries so you can automatically connect to servers via modem. To create a call entry:

1. Using the Location button on the status bar, select a location where you need to use a modem to connect to the server. Home or Hotel are possible settings.
2. Click the entry that you want to appear immediately below your call entry.
3. Choose Create, Call Entry.
4. (Optional) By default, the call entry specifies your home server. To specify a different server, double-click the call entry action button; select the server you want to call, and then click OK.

Once your replication tasks are complete, you need to disconnect the modem from the telephone line. A hangup entry will do this automatically for you.

To create a hangup entry:

1. Using the Location button on the status bar, select a location where you need to use a modem to connect to the server.

2. Click the entry you want to appear immediately below the hangup entry (you can always move the entry if you get it in the wrong place).
3. Choose Create, Hangup Entry. A hangup entry appears on the Replicator page.

Even if you have more than one call entry, you only need one hangup entry. The Replicator hangs up automatically from the first call entry when it encounters a new call entry, so you only need to hang up after the final call.

USING SEND/RECEIVE MAIL

Before you leave the office to go on the road, make sure:

- Your location and connection documents are set up.
- Your replicas are created and you've added any necessary entries to the Replicator page.
- You have a phone cord, extra battery packs, and a power adapter.
- You have the phone number for your Notes administrator.
- You've loaded Help Lite if you don't already have the Help database on your computer.

To send and receive mail while working remotely:

1. Plug one end of the phone cord into your modem's port and the other into a phone jack on the wall or on the back of a phone.
2. Make sure you disable call waiting on that line, or it will disconnect you from the server (try dialing *70).
3. Click the Location button on the status bar and choose your current location, if it's not already selected.
4. If you're not on the Replicator page, click the Replicator tab. Then choose one of the following methods:

- Choose Actions, Send and Receive Mail.
- Click the Send & Receive Mail button on the Action bar.
- Choose Actions, Send Outgoing Mail (to send mail only).

Notes initializes the modem and the call goes out to your home server. Your new mail will be replicated to the server and the server will replicate any new mail to your computer. Once replication is complete, your computer hangs up. If you want to stop the mail from being sent or the replication process, click Stop. Once you're back in the office, remember to switch your location back to one for connection to the network.

Because you are keeping a local replica and the hard disk space on your laptop might be limited, you want to delete old mail frequently to keep your Mail database at a manageable size.

You may also need to compact your databases to get rid of the empty spaces left by the deleted files. To do this:

1. Double-click the Workspace tab.
2. Click the Information tab on the Properties box (see Figure 25.2).

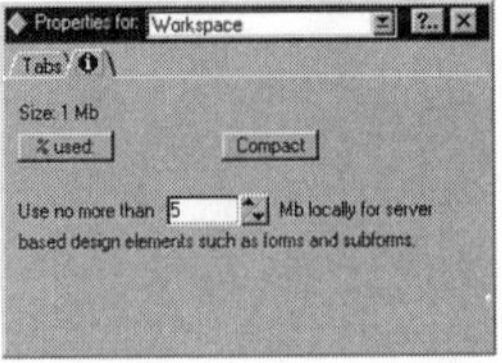

FIGURE 25.2 The Information page of the Properties box.

3. In the Properties box, select Workspace from the drop-down list; then click the % used button.
4. If the percentage is under 85%, click the Compact button.

In this lesson, you learned about how mobile Mail differs from online Mail and how to replicate your Mail database. In the next lesson, you learn how to configure the Replicator page.

Configuring the Replicator Page

In this lesson, you learn how to use the replicator page and how to configure it by adding call, hangup, and database entries.

If you are a remote user who replicates databases in addition to your Mail database, you'll find this lesson very useful.

What Is the Replicator Page?

The Replicator page is the last page of your workspace, and it's the one workspace tab that you can't delete. The Replicator page provides a central location to handle all your replication needs. Using the features available on the Replicator page (see Figure 26.1), you can set options to control which databases replicate, which servers you are replicating with, and whether you want to receive full or truncated (shortened) documents when you replicate.

There are several rows, or *entries*, on the Replicator page:

Start Replication at   Sets a schedule for replication; you can't delete or move this entry. Most people do not schedule their replications, since that would require that you turn on your PC and run Notes during the scheduled time. You'll usually use replication on demand, so you don't need to set this option.

Send outgoing mail   Sends all pending messages from your mailbox. For each local database replica you have, there is a database entry on the Replicator page. You can select which databases you want to replicate in a particular session. To replicate only one database, click its entry to select it. Then click the Other Actions button on the Action bar and choose Replicate selected database.

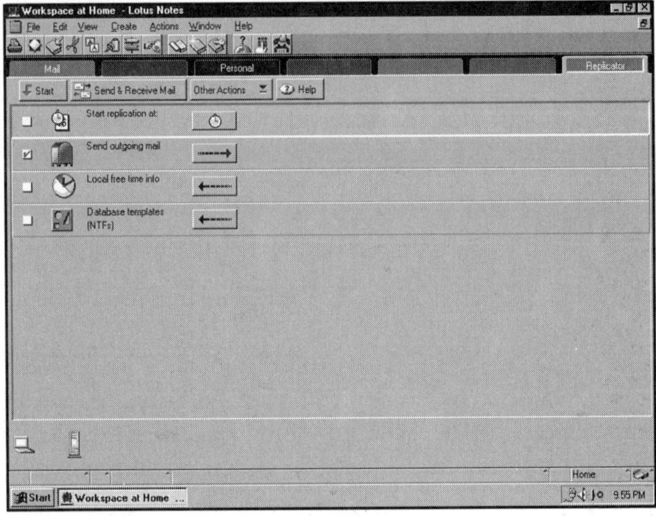

FIGURE 26.1 The Replicator page.

Database templates Refreshes the designs of any template-based databases you have. You can't delete this entry.

Call and Hangup In addition to the automatic entry rows, you can create Call and Hangup entries for mobile locations.

On many of the entry rows, you see action buttons. Use these to specify replication options relating to that entry row.

Each entry row also has a check box. To select an entry, click the check box (a check mark appears). When you click the Start button on the Action bar, Lotus Notes performs the functions of each checked entry row in the order of the rows.

The status bar at the bottom of the page shows information about the current replication, letting you know when Lotus Notes is attempting to call a server, what database is being replicated, the progress of the replication, how many minutes are left, and when the replication is finished. After replication, the status bar displays statistics for individual entries.

Setting Replication Priority

You can set a replication priority for a database entry on the Replicator page. Select the database entry and click it once with the right mouse button. Choose High priority from the menu; an exclamation point appears on high priority database entries. When you want to replicate high priority databases, click the Other Actions button on the Action bar, and select Replicate high priority databases from the menu.

Configuring the Replicator Page

Except for a couple of the fixed entries on the Replicator page, you can move and delete entries to suit your needs.

To delete entries:

1. Click the entry you want to delete. This selects the entry.
2. Press Delete.
3. When asked if you want to delete the entry, select Yes.

Be careful about deleting database entries. When you delete an entry from the Replicator page, it also deletes the database from all locations. Instead of deleting the entry, remove the check mark to deselect it from the replication process.

Lotus Notes replicates the databases in the order they appear on the Replicator page. To move an entry:

1. Click the entry and hold down the mouse button.
2. Drag the entry to the position where you want it.
3. Release the mouse button.

Making Call and Hangup Entries

If you are a mobile user, you'll want to create call entries so you can automatically connect to servers via modem. To create a call entry:

1. Using the Location button on the status bar, select a location where you need to use a modem to connect to the server. Home or Hotel are possible settings.
2. Click the entry that you want to appear immediately below your call entry.
3. Choose Create, Call Entry.

   (Optional) By default, the call entry specifies your home server. To specify a different server, double-click the call entry action button; select the server you want to call, and then click OK. The list of servers that appears only includes those servers that have specified telephone numbers. If you need to add another server to the list or have to change a telephone number, choose File, Mobile, Server Phone Numbers.

Once your replication tasks are complete, you need to disconnect the modem from the telephone line. A hangup entry will do this automatically for you.

To create a hangup entry:

1. Using the Location button on the status bar, select a location where you need to use a modem to connect to the server.
2. Click the entry you want to appear immediately below the hangup entry (you can always move the entry if you get it in the wrong place).
3. Choose Create, Hangup Entry.

Even if you have more than one call entry, you only need one hangup entry. The Replicator hangs up automatically from the first call entry when it encounters a new call entry, so you only need to hang up after the final call.

ADDING DATABASES

When you add a new replica to your workspace, Lotus Notes automatically adds the database entry to your Replicator page. You can then delete the database entries you don't want to appear there.

However, if you delete a database entry and want to put it back on the Replicator page, click the database icon on your workspace and then drag it to the Replicator tab. Then move the entry to an appropriate position on the page.

Instead of deleting a database and having to put it back later, it may be easier to temporarily disable it. This is a particularly good idea if you think the database might be corrupt, and you don't want to replicate it with the server until you check it out. To temporarily disable a database:

1. Click the right mouse button on the database icon on the workspace or on the database entry on the Replicator page.
2. Choose Replication Settings.
3. In the Replication Settings dialog box (see Figure 26.2), click Other.

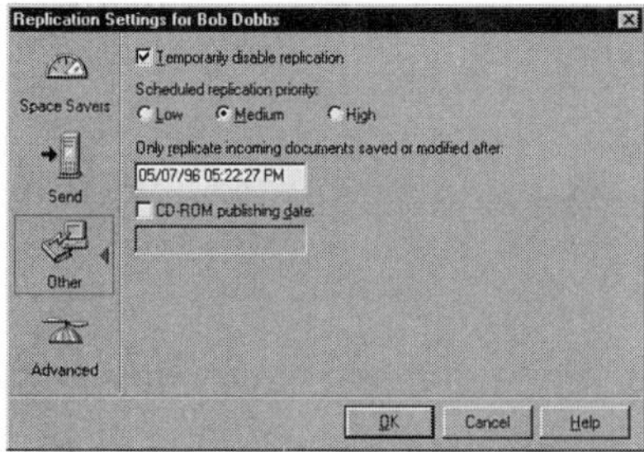

FIGURE 26.2 The Replication Settings dialog box.

4. Check Temporarily disable replication.
5. Click OK.

CONFIGURING FOR SEVERAL SERVERS

You can specify which server to use when replicating a particular database.

1. Click the database entry action button. The arrow on the button shows the current direction in which the database replicates. The Replication dialog box appears, as shown in Figure 26.3.

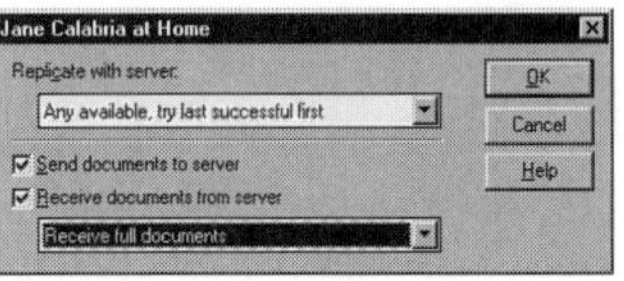

FIGURE 26.3 The Replication dialog box.

2. Under Replicate with server, choose one of these options:

   Any available, try last successful first Tries to replicate first with the server with which you last replicated, and then tries with any available server it can find.

   Any available, try Server Name first Tries to replicate first with the server specified, and then tries with any available server it can find.

   Server Name Lets you choose that specific server name.

3. Select what you want to replicate by checking Send documents to server and/or Receive documents from server.

4. When you choose to receive documents from the server, select one of the options from the list box: Receive full documents, Receive summary and 40K of rich text only, or Receive summary only. The summary includes only basic information such as the author and subject.

5. Click OK.

If you choose to receive less than the full documents, it doesn't mean you can't get the whole document later.

1. Open the document for which you need the complete text, or select several documents.
2. Choose Actions, Retrieve Entire Document.
3. Select Get documents now via background.
4. Click OK.
5. If more than one server has the full text, Lotus Notes prompts you to pick the server from which you want to retrieve it.

USING SELECTIVE REPLICATION

In addition to limiting the replication of documents to only the summary or to the summary plus only 40K of rich text, there are other methods for limiting what part of a database you replicate. When you are working remotely, reduce the time allotted for replication, and save on telephone charges.

Many of the options you have in replicating databases are in the Replication Settings dialog box (see Figure 26.4), which you can access by clicking on the database entry with the right mouse button and then selecting Replication Settings from the menu.

Use the following settings to limit what you replicate in the selected database:

- With the Space Savers icon selected, check Remove documents not modified in the last and specify the number of days. This purges old documents from your replica.
- To receive only selected folders and views, check Replicate a subset of documents. Then select one or more folders and views.
- To receive only selected documents, check Replicate a subset of documents. Check Select by formula. Enter the formula. *Do not attempt this if you are unfamiliar with Lotus Notes formulas.*

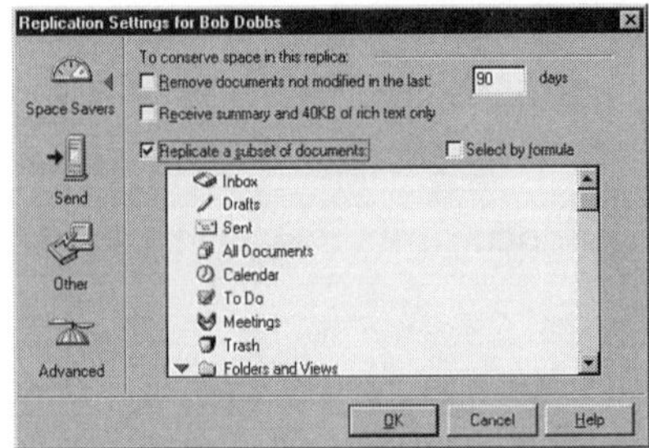

FIGURE 26.4 The Replication Settings dialog box with Space Savers icon selected.

- Click the Send icon and check Do not send deletions made in this replica to other replicas so you don't replicate documents you have deleted from the replica since the replica's last purge interval.
- With the Send icon selected, check Do not send changes in database title & catalog info to other replicas so you don't replicate any changes to anyone else that you made to the database title or database catalog entry for your replica.
- Also on the Send page, check Do not send changes in local security property to other replicas so you don't pass on changes you made to the security settings on your replica.
- With the Other icon selected, enter a cutoff date in the box below Only replicate incoming documents saved or modified after. This guarantees that you will only receive recent documents, and it doesn't purge old documents from the database.
- With the Other icon selected, enter a cutoff date in the box below Only replicate incoming documents saved or modified after. This guarantees that you will only receive recent documents, and it doesn't purge old documents from the database.

- To receive only selected portions of the database's design, click the Advanced icon (see Figure 26.5). Check Forms, views, and so on. Check Agents to get only the database agents or Access control list to receive the ACL. Check Replication formula to receive the formula the database uses to select the documents it receives.
- Also on the Advanced page, check Deletions to remove any documents from your replica that have already been deleted from the source database.

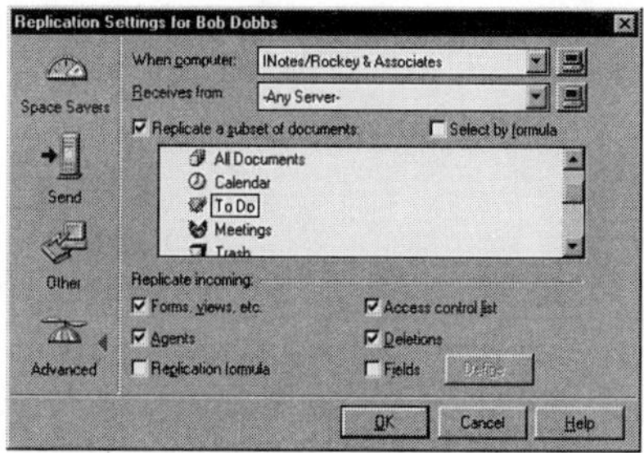

FIGURE 26.5 The Replication Settings dialog box with the Advanced icon selected.

In this lesson, you learned how to configure the Replicator page and how to use selective replication.

INDEX

A

D

E

F–G

H

I–K

L

O

P–Q

S

T

U

V